DELOITTE & CO.

1845–1956

DELOITTE
& CO.

1845-1956

Printed privately for

DELOITTE, PLENDER, GRIFFITHS & CO.

at the UNIVERSITY PRESS, OXFORD

C

PRINTED IN GREAT BRITAIN

To all those who have been
'with Deloittes'

CONTENTS

ILLUSTRATIONS

NOTE

by SIR RUSSELL KETTLE

A FEW years ago I suggested to Mr. Kilpatrick that he should expand his fascinating brochure *Some Notes on the Early Days of the Firm* to cover the story of the firm from its foundation in 1845 to date. This he readily agreed to do. Unfortunately after he had collected a certain amount of material ill health forced him to relinquish his partnership and he felt unable to proceed with the task, which, with his literary turn of mind, he was so well qualified to undertake. In stepping into the breach I have, with Mr. Kilpatrick's consent, made free use of the contents of his brochure and of other data assembled by him, particularly relating to the early period of the firm's existence. I am grateful to him, to my former partners, and to past and present members of the staff for the help they have given me in reviewing the contemporary scenes, personalities, and events during the 112 years which have passed since W. W. Deloitte set up his plate in Basinghall Street.

July 1957

DELOITTE & CO.

W. W. DELOITTE
  11, Basinghall Street, E.C.   1845–55
  4, Lothbury, E.C.   1855–7

DELOITTE & GREENWOOD
  4, Lothbury, E.C.   1857–62

DELOITTE, GREENWOOD & DEVER
  4, Lothbury, E.C.   1862–7

DELOITTE, DEVER, HOLLEBONE & CO.
  4, Lothbury, E.C.   1867–9

DELOITTE, DEVER, HOLLEBONE & GRIFFITHS
  4, Lothbury, E.C.   1869–73

DELOITTE, DEVER, GRIFFITHS & CO.
  4, Lothbury, E.C.   1873–1905

DELOITTE, PLENDER, GRIFFITHS & CO.
  5, London Wall Buildings, E.C. 2   1905–

PARTNERS IN LONDON FIRM

BROUGHT DOWN TO JUNE 1957

WILLIAM WELCH DELOITTE
1845–97
President, Institute of Chartered Accountants 1888–1889

THOMAS GREENWOOD 1857–67

HENRY DEVER 1862–97

ALFRED R. HOLLEBONE 1867–73

JOHN G. GRIFFITHS 1869–1902
President, Institute of Chartered Accountants 1897–1899; M.V.O. 1916; C.V.O. 1917

GEORGE CLOUTTE 1889–1904

WILLIAM PLENDER 1897–1946
President, Institute of Chartered Accountants 1910–1912 and 1929–1930; Knighted 1911; G.B.E. 1918; Baronet 1923; Baron 1931

PERCIVAL D. GRIFFITHS
1898–1937

EDWARD DAVIS 1902–19

LIONEL MALTBY 1902–36

HERBERT GUEDALLA 1902–11

HARRY I. CHEVALIER 1907–17

ARTHUR E. CUTFORTH 1912–39
President, Institute of Chartered Accountants 1934–1936; C.B.E. 1926; Knighted 1938

ROBERT KERR 1918

RICHARD C. MARTIN 1918–34

RUSSELL KETTLE 1919–55
President, Institute of Chartered Accountants 1949–1950; Knighted 1947

ALAN RAE SMITH 1919–56
Knighted 1935; K.B.E. 1948

HAROLD READ 1921–47

JAMES KILPATRICK 1925–53

HAROLD HOCKLEY 1925–50

JOHN W. BAIRD 1931–42

CHARLES R. GOULDER 1934–

FRANK A. LORD 1942–

JOHN GODFREY, M.A. 1942–

W. GUY DENSEM 1946–

LAURENCE J. CULSHAW 1946–

ROBERT T. M. McPHAIL, M.B.E.
1947–

A. WILFRED SARSON 1948–

VERNON A. TUDBALL 1949–

CHARLES ROMER-LEE, M.A.
1949–

GORDON E. MORRISH 1950–

RONALD F. GEORGE, T.D. 1952–

DAVID D. RAE SMITH, M.C., B.A.
1954–

STANLEY P. WILKINS 1954–

J. NESS PRENTICE, M.B.E., B.A.
1957–

RICHARD KETTLE, B.A. 1957–

On pages 147 to 160 will be found particulars of other offices of Deloitte & Co. and associated Deloitte firms and their resident partners

The Period 1845–1900

WILLIAM WELCH DELOITTE, the founder of the firm, set up in practice at the age of 27 as a public accountant in the City of London in 1845, eight years after Queen Victoria had ascended the throne. Some aspects of the contemporary scene have been portrayed by Mr. Kilpatrick in *Some Notes on the Early Days of the Firm*:

Sir Robert Peel was Prime Minister and a rising young Member of Parliament, William Ewart Gladstone, was President of the Board of Trade. Dickens was at the height of his powers, Carlyle, Macaulay, Tennyson, Landseer, Disraeli, Thackeray, Browning, all the great Victorians were alive; gas lighting was being extended in London, and we read of its appearance in the Bank of England in 1843; the railway boom had come and gone and the early railway companies were beginning to prosper, to pave the way for the great railway mania of 1845; the steel pen was gradually supplanting the quill; envelopes were practically unknown and letters were sealed by wafers; public execution was a form of entertainment; most Londoners walked to their offices or places of business, and it is stated that in 1837 90,000 persons crossed London Bridge daily, as a means of conveyance within the city boundaries practically did not exist.

England was entering upon the latter phase of the Industrial Revolution, with the trade slumps and periodic fluctuations which are often associated with a too rapidly expanding economy.

It was a time of robust, if harsh, economic development. The increase of the population of the United Kingdom between 1841 and 1851 by over $2\frac{1}{4}$ millions to about 22 millions was accompanied by a swelling exodus from the countryside into the industrial towns; by 1851 about one-half of the population was urban and the personal employer, increasingly unable to provide sufficient capital in an enlarged market, was meeting a new competitor in the joint stock company. Within those ten years the economy changed from regional to national and this transformation was attributable in large measure to the rapid improvement in the means of transport and communication. The construction of railways linked the countryside, ports, and coalfields with the growing centres of population and industry. In 1842 the voyage by iron steamship between the old world and the new had been reduced from one month to twelve days: penny post had been introduced in 1840 and public telegraph in 1843. Mr. Nicholas A. H. Stacey, in his interesting study *English Accountancy—1800–1954*, has depicted the conditions at the beginning of the second half of the nineteenth century which favoured and foreshadowed the subsequent progress of accountancy as a profession:

Leaving behind the turbulent 40's with their famines, unrest, political and social mutations, Britain had entered with the commencement of the second half of the nineteenth century one of the most prosperous and peaceful periods in her history. Since the Congress of Vienna, Britain had fought no wars, save the Crimea expedition, nor had her immediate neighbours on the continent of Europe. Peace is a stimulant to development. The world's trade centred on Britain; she became the world's workshop, banker and clearing house for transit trade. This period may be termed as the first honeymoon of fully grown industrial capitalism. The prosperity of the mid-nineteenth century was as much due to scientific improvement as to the result of social and political reforms effected in the twenty years preceding it. Both these fortuitous circumstances were coupled with the uniquely enlarged absorbing capacity of overseas markets. Exports rose rapidly and the bulk of the exports was destined for foreign countries, as against the Empire in later days. It requires little imagination to perceive the upswing in the need for accountants in auditing, banking, bankruptcy, and financial accountancy and subsequently in cost accountancy. No wonder that some three associations of accountants were formed in Scotland quickly in succession at the commencement of the second half of the nineteenth century. In England an accountancy society was not to see the light of day until 1870.

And it was in 1842 that the first Income Tax was introduced, which was intended to be of a temporary character.

Accountancy in 1845

The London Post Office directory of 1845 shows that there were 205 firms of accountants practising in the City of London, the leading firm being Quilter & Ball; nearly three-quarters of a century later their practice, then carried on under the name of Welton & Bond, was absorbed by Deloittes. When accountancy in England took on the semblance of an organized profession in 1870 and for many years thereafter, an accountant was mainly dependent upon insolvency work, and this association with the often sordid circumstances of bankruptcy proceedings tended to lower his standing in the estimation of the public. We read of Deloitte's clerk attending at Newgate prison to collect information from a bankrupt. Many of the firms then in existence combined their accountancy work with other occupations such as estate agents, valuers, and auctioneers.

3

Before Deloitte set up as an accountant he had spent twelve years on the staff of the Official Assignee in Bankruptcy of the City of London and had thus gained valuable experience in the branch of accountancy which then and for many years predominated over all others. He took an office at 11, Basinghall Street close to that of his former employer, and no doubt his choice of this address was not wholly disinterested. His first Time Ledger, the only surviving record of his earliest activities, covers the period from April 1845 to May 1846 and is now exhibited in the firm's reception office. It begins with an entry in Deloitte's own handwriting under date 23 April 1845 recording $1\frac{1}{2}$ hours spent by his clerk, Mr. Copley, on the affairs of a Mr. Albert Green: the time so occupied appears to have been of an exploratory nature for we find that after Deloitte himself had given $1\frac{1}{2}$ hours to the matter on 29 April the account was closed. Mr. Copley must surely be the precursor of the long line of members of the staff who have served the firm so faithfully and so well. In all, the Time Ledger contains the names of ninety-seven clients of whom eighty-two were individuals, fourteen were partnerships, and one—quite surprisingly—the Cirencester Savings Bank; but it must be admitted that this impressive number of clients collected by Deloitte in such a comparatively short space of time included many small and trivial engagements. Except in one instance—Mr. E. Smith, an auctioneer—there is no clue to the occupations of the clients other than the savings bank: we shall never know whether the account headed 'Mr. Rothschild' indicated the famous banking house in St. Swithins Lane. The names of no less than eighteen clerks appear, but of

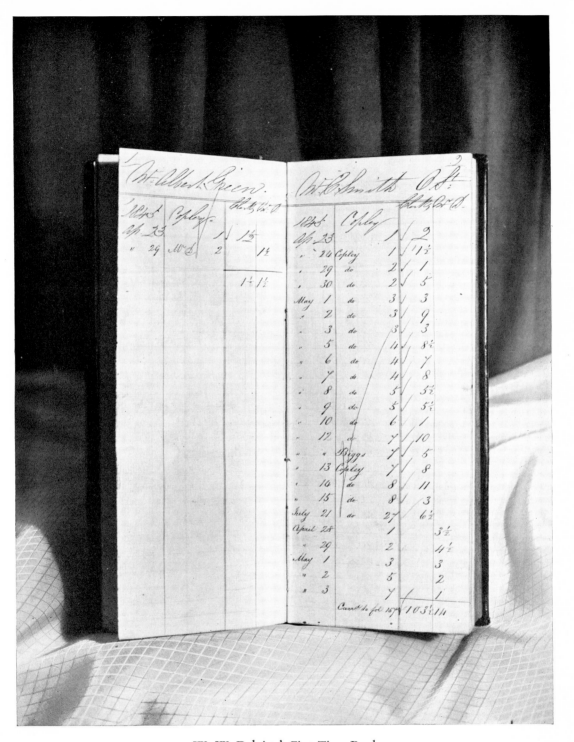

W. W. Deloitte's First Time Book

'Baton' issued to Staff in early years of the firm

these we suspect many were employed temporarily: however, in a letter written by Deloitte's grandmother in 1847 she proudly refers to the fact that her grandson was employing a staff of ten in Basinghall Street. Clerks did not then undergo the training or possess the qualifications now requisite and no doubt their re-muneration was modest. They worked longer hours: the Time Ledger suggests that a 9-hour day was normal and shows that on occasions, no doubt in times of urgency, from 10 to 17 hours were worked daily. On many matters Deloitte himself was occupied each day and it may be that these were insolvencies de-manding a greater amount of his personal attention: in 1846 bankruptcies were abnormally high.

Audit clerks were given, as part of their equipment, a 'Baton'. It had three compartments: the larger one held pens and coloured lead pencils and of the other two compartments, the inner one contained a bottle of ink and the outer one india-rubbers.

Early recollections of W. W. Deloitte

Another glimpse of Deloitte from the past has been provided by the late John Gane.[1]

I retain a vivid recollection of Mr. Deloitte when, early in January 1857 he engaged me, a lad under sixteen years of age, as his junior clerk at a salary of nothing per annum.

Articles were not then in fashion, and learners had to do without remuneration for a time, and to be content with small salaries sub-sequently. [*One letter in the office letter book reads: 'We consider that your services for the first 12 months would be amply remunerated by what you would learn in that time.'*]

[1] John Gane left Deloittes in 1870 to practice in partnership with Herbert Jackson, also a former member of the staff, in the firm known today as Gane, Jackson, Jefferys & Freeman.

Mr. Deloitte was an alert, decisive little man, with just a touch of austerity in his manner; this, however, covered a kind heart. He was most particular in all things and dressed very carefully.

I have reason for believing that his patience was sorely tried for a while by the inability of his new junior clerk to make head or tail of his handwriting. There were no stenographers, typists, or press copy books in those days, consequently it was the custom for principals to write all letters personally and for the clerk to copy them, by hand, in a specially bound book. A part of my duty was the latter operation wherein my troubles were many and grievous, for Mr. Deloitte's writing was of too distinguished a character to be readily readable by a youth fresh from the imitation of copperplate.

At the time I mention Mr. Deloitte had no partner, but his energy enabled him to carry on a considerable business, assisted as he was by Mr. Henry Dever, then his managing clerk.

Henry Dever as well as John Gane copied numerous letters in the bound letter books and such letters were marked and initialed 'Posted—or delivered—by me'.

W. W. Deloitte's professional career and personal qualities

From such small beginnings there emerged over the years the firm known today as Deloitte, Plender, Griffiths & Co. and its associated firms overseas. Deloitte himself had the satisfaction of seeing the firm he founded securely established in England during the fifty-two years he presided over its destinies. He retired in 1897 at the age of 79, one year before his death, and with the passing of the years he has become a legendary figure in the annals of the firm. We turn for a contemporary assessment of his professional standing and personal qualities to his obituary notice in *The Accountant*:

He had probably been in business longer than any other accountant and at the time of his retirement from his firm he was the oldest practising accountant living. For many years he and his firm had been widely and honourably known, and have had the handling of large and important matters.

To mention all would occupy far too much space, but it may be said that the present system of keeping English Railway Accounts is due very largely to Mr. Deloitte's initiative in the eighteen-sixties when he acted as professional accountant to the Great Western Railway. He was also the originator of a system of Hotel Account-keeping which is now universally adopted by all large hotels at home and abroad; and it will be well remembered by the older members of the profession that he investigated and unravelled the great frauds that were perpetrated on the Great Northern Railway by Redpath in 1857, and on the Great Eastern Steamship Company in 1870. Mr. Deloitte was closely associated with the late Sir John Pender, Sir Richard Glass, Sir George Elliott, Sir Daniel Gooch, Mr. Cyrus Field and the other pioneers of submarine telegraphy, and his firm have had continuously the audit of nearly all the large cable companies.

Mr. Deloitte took great interest in the formation of the Institute of Chartered Accountants. He was a member of the Council of the old Institute of Accountants, and on its absorption by the Institute of Chartered Accountants he took a seat on the Council with one of his partners, Mr. John G. Griffiths, the present President. Mr. Deloitte was Vice-President for the four years 1884–88, and in 1889 he was elected President. He also took great interest in, and was one of the founders of the Chartered Accountants' Benevolent Association, and until his retirement from business held the office of President. He was also a member of the old Manchester Society of Accountants, and many years ago carried on business there, the firm being Deloitte & Halliday. [*This was a branch office.*]

He was proud of the profession to which he belonged, and noted with increasing interest the improved status of its members before the public.

Some of the best-known stockbrokers and accountants and other professional men have passed through his office, which has long been recognised as one of the nurseries of the profession.

Mr. Deloitte was a very old Freemason, having been a member of the craft for upwards of fifty years.

He delighted in the pleasures of a country life, and for the last forty years had lived at Southall, in Middlesex, where he held considerable property. He was of a generous disposition, and, in addition to building a church at Southall, he erected, in Jubilee year, a number of alms-houses for the poor.

He was a man of great determination, sound judgment, and exceptional business ability.

The oil painting of W. W. Deloitte which hangs in the reception room in London Office was recently acquired from the church at Southall.

Origin of the name 'Deloitte': his ancestry and habits

The derivation of the name 'Deloitte' has frequently aroused curiosity amongst the firm's clients. We are indebted to the late Edward Allbeury, who was a nephew of Deloitte and bore a strong likeness to his uncle, and who joined the staff in 1879, for the following particulars of his uncle's ancestry, early life, and habits.

Mr. Deloitte was the grandson of a certain Count de Loitte, who held an important position in the household of Louis XVI. In the Reign of Terror in 1793 Count de Loitte managed to reach the coast of France and, bribing some fishermen to take him to England, he eventually landed at Hull, his sole possession being some jewellery. He was fortunate in obtaining an appointment as Professor of French at a college in Hull, and about a year afterwards he married the daughter of a leading county family.

Mr. Deloitte's father (one of the sons of the Count) was secretary to a then well-known firm of provision merchants, and lived in Great Dover

Basinghall Street, showing site of first office
(No. 11 is opposite the parked car)

The Royal Exchange in the heart of the City originally built in 1566, rebuilt in 1842–4. In the pediment the financial and business community are reminded that 'The Earth is the Lord's and the Fulness thereof'

(*Fox Photos Ltd.*)

Street, S.E., which was then a residential district. He married the daughter of a West Indies planter named Welch, and I understand that her dowry consisted of a number of slaves.

Our Mr. Deloitte went to a day school within easy walking distance of his home. In those days boys left school at an early age, but he left at the age of fifteen obtaining a position as assistant to a Mr. Edwards who was Official Assignee at the Bankruptcy Court. After a few years Mr. Deloitte started in practice at 11, Basinghall Street at the age of twenty-seven, and lived over the office. He married at twenty-one. No doubt, Mr. Edwards, knowing his aptitude for accounts, helped him very considerably by giving him work, as did also at a later date a Mr. Richard Glass (a schoolmate), who was a partner in the firm of Glass, Elliott & Co., engineers and cable manufacturers.

After a time Mr. Deloitte got tired of living over his office with his wife, and they went to live at Fulham. (He was married twice, the second marriage taking place about 1860.) In or about 1858 he bought a farm-house with considerable land attached (Hill House, Southall) and at considerable expense converted it into a comfortable house and made gardens, lawns, etc. of some acres; he kept two Jersey cows, some sheep, pigs and poultry. Also a horse for his brougham and two ponies for a phaeton in the summer.

He was very peculiar in some respects. He would get home soon after six and go to bed about ten. He would smoke one cigar in the evening, and more often than not would not say one single word during the whole evening, but would not miss a single word of the conversation going on, so I, amongst others, had to be very careful.

Sunday was open house. A train arrived at Southall from Paddington at two-thirty, and dinner was at three. It was never known how many would arrive unexpectedly, and catering was thus difficult. He kept a cellar of choice wines and fine cigars which his guests thoroughly enjoyed. [*In May 1857 there is a letter written from the office ordering 12 doz. port at 48/- per dozen 'if you cannot do so at a less price'.*]

I think I am about the only one left who participated in these dinners. Amongst frequent guests were Mr. and Mrs. Dever, Mr. and

9

Mrs. J. G. Griffiths, Mr. Dubois (Mrs. J. G. Griffiths' father), and Mr. Dubois (Mrs. J. G. Griffiths' brother).

His usual drink was sherry, of which he was considered a good judge. He never gambled or played cards, and thought billiards a wicked game. He had no particular hobby and went in for no sport as a young man except for a very occasional game of cricket.

When he began to enjoy an increased income he seems to have taken to driving and spent some little time each day in Hyde Park. He was very proud of two pedigree ponies, which had belonged to the well-known Lola Montez.

He was noted for wearing a choice flower in his buttonhole every day, both in summer and winter, and his gardener must have had some trouble to meet his daily demand.

Deloitte's grandfather, the Count, evidently thought it more appropriate to his reduced circumstances and in the then existing state of national feeling towards France to drop his title and anglicize his name, for we find an entry in the Hull directory of that period 'Deloitte, J. O. C.—Teacher of the French Language'. The change was not confined to his surname: in other documents 'Jean Onuphre Noailles' becomes 'John Onuphre Christmas'! There are still to be found in the Belgian Ardennes two villages called Louette St. Denis and Louette St. Pierre—shown on old maps as Loit or Loitte Grand and Petit—where the Count had his estates and was once Seigneur of the Manor. Mr. Allbeury's son, a great-great-grandson of Count de Loitte, is still on the staff at 5, London Wall Buildings, thus spanning a period of service of father and son of over seventy-seven years, except for an absence of the former in 1898 for a few months in Brazil as accountant to one of the firm's clients. There is now only one known living descendant of the Count bearing his name—Miss

Enid Marley Deloitte, a great-grand-daughter, of Sydney, N.S.W., where her late father's firm of insurance brokers still carries on business as Deloitte & Walker.

Early methods of securing business

It is to be feared that Deloitte's keenness as a young practitioner led him to seek clients by methods which would not satisfy today's professional code of conduct. But *autres temps, autres mœurs*, and he was doing nothing which would appear unethical or unjustified to himself or his competitors. In the only surviving letter book of those early days (1854–8) we find such an approach:

I am sorry to see your name in the Gazette, and write to offer my services to prepare your Balance Sheet for the Court. You may rely on my doing anything for you in my power.

And again:

Mr. G. Elliott informs me an Accountant will be required to examine the Books and Accounts of Lady Londonderry, and at his recommendation I enclose my card and beg to offer my services for that purpose. I am Accountant to the Auditors of the Great Western, Lancashire & Yorkshire, South Wales and other important railway companies, which I hope will be considered sufficient guarantee of my integrity and qualifications. I can obtain testimonials of the very highest character. Awaiting your answer.

The latter letter was written to a Mr. R. Anderson of Seaham Harbour, Durham, to which undertaking, then owned by the Londonderry family, the firm has acted as auditors for many years, and it may be that the connexion emanated from this correspondence. We do not know whether testimonials were called for and submitted, but it seems clear from a portion of a lithographed document which has recently come to light that Deloitte was helped by credentials obtained from his friends.

4, Lothbury

The business grew rapidly and in 1855 Deloitte moved to larger offices at 4, Lothbury, within a stone's throw of the Bank of England, at an annual rental of £140.

In *Some Notes on the Early Days of the Firm* Mr. Kilpatrick writes:

Being somewhat curious to discover the origin of the names Basinghall and Lothbury, I made some inquiries and learned that the former took its name from the Basing family, who lived in the vicinity from the reign of John to that of Edward III. On the north side of the Bank of England was the district where the pewterers and candlestick-makers and other workers in metal carried on their trade. Founders' Court takes its name from the brassfounders and Tokenhouse Yard from the manufacture of 'tokens', the copper coinage in use in England up to the middle of the seventeenth century. Lothbury is said to have derived its name from the loathsome noise and smell caused by those metal workers in the exercise of their trade.

A narrow passage led out of Copthall Avenue, emerging through a building into Tokenhouse Yard. A thin iron column divided the low entrance at this end so that one had to walk almost sideways to emerge; the object was said to be to bar the escape of highwaymen on horseback. This iron bar, corroded with long exposure, was removed in recent years, presumably in the interests of speed. There must still be many who remember it and regret the disappearance of yet another relic of the medieval city.

4, Lothbury in 1905

(The entrance to the office was the first door to the left of the main entrance)

The Bank of England, 1854

(By permission of the Director, Guildhall Art Gallery)

From contemporary evidence it appears that Deloitte's early success was largely due to recognition of his outstanding abilities as an accountant by a group of leading industrialists, chief amongst whom were those already referred to, all of whom subsequently had titles bestowed upon them by the Queen, namely Richard Glass, George Elliott, Daniel Gooch, and John Pender. Between them they were associated with a variety of important undertakings, remarkable in number and spread over the whole country, including railways, docks, collieries, and ironworks, to many of which Deloitte was appointed auditor. Up to 1844 limited liability was normally obtainable only by private Act of Parliament. In that year the first Companies Act enabled companies to secure legal status, but the privilege of limited liability was first conceded by the Companies Act 1855. Under the Act of 1844 the independent audit of a company's accounts was made compulsory, but this requirement was dropped from the Companies Act 1862 and not re-enacted, except in relation to banks, until 1900. Nevertheless, Richard Brown, C.A., in his *History of Accounting and Accountants*, published in 1905, says: 'The Companies Act 1862 may be termed the accountant's friend, for it provides him with an occupation (and incidentally with remuneration) at the inception, during the progress and in the liquidation of public companies.' The number of company registrations following the Act of 1862 was phenomenal: added impetus was no doubt given by the prohibition, still in force at the present day, of partnerships of more than twenty persons. The reason for this restriction, as explained in a judgement of the Court of Appeal some years later, was '. . . to prevent the mischief arising from large trading undertakings being carried on by large fluctuating bodies, so that persons dealing with them did not know with whom they were contracting, and so might be put to great difficulty and expense, which was a public mischief to be repressed'.

Some clients of long standing

Several companies are mentioned in the old letter book which are still clients of the firm, for instance, The Ouvah Coffee Co. Ltd. (now Ouvah Ceylon Estates Ltd.), the Powell Duffryn Steam Coal Co. Ltd. (which took over the business of Thomas Powell and is now Powell Duffryn Ltd.), the Telegraph Construction & Maintenance Co. Ltd., and the Vulcan Foundry Co. Ltd. These were all registered in 1864 but were in being earlier, the Vulcan Foundry having been founded by the father of railways, George Stephenson, in 1830.

The minute of the board of the Powell Duffryn Company appointing the firm as auditors in 1864 read:

That Messrs. Deloitte & Co. be the first and present auditors and their remuneration being hereafter fixed and their duties for the present being to effect an audit of the accounts from the first of January up to this time and to continue such audit regularly by means of monthly visits of Mr. Deloitte himself and such other means as he finds needful.

The growth of the firm's connexion in South Wales necessitated within a few years a resident staff in Cardiff and it is to be hoped that Deloitte was relieved from his monthly visit. It was, however, not until 1912 that a branch office was opened there and a little later at Swansea.

It is only in recent years that the description 'Consulting Accountants' has come into vogue. It may therefore be a matter of surprise to read the minute passed by the board of the Telegraph Construction & Maintenance Co. Ltd. in 1864: 'Resolved that Messrs. Deloitte, Greenwood & Dever be appointed Consulting Accountants to the Company.'

Other early clients to whom reference is made were the London & River Plate Bank (now merged in the Bank of London and South America) and the Ocean Coal Co. Ltd.

Basis of firm's charges

The earliest accounts of the firm which have escaped destruction are those for the first period in which Deloitte took a partner, namely the half-year to 30 September 1857, so that we possess no information about fees, salaries, and other expenses and profits whilst Deloitte practised on his own account. But time employed plus expenses was then, as now, the basis of charge and we find Deloitte writing to a solicitor in Colchester in May 1855: 'I received your letter of the 23rd instant and beg to inform you in answer that my charge will be £3. 3. 0. per day for self, and £1. 11. 6. per day for clerk, including expenses, with the exception of railway fare each way in addition.' In September 1855 we find a reference to remuneration in what must surely have been the first prospectus work:

You are quite at liberty to print my name as your Auditor describing me as of 4, Lothbury, that being my present address. With regard to the remuneration I shall expect to be paid a fair sum according to the time employed. Please send me one of your Prospectuses as soon as they are ready.

A complaint against charges by a client brought forth the following somewhat aggressive reply:

15

I received your letter of the 9th instant. I presume you are a sufficient man of business to know the difference between a conversation as to the probable cost of making up your accounts and a contract to do so at a certain price which certainly was not done on my behalf as such is not my practice.

The accounts were as you must be aware far heavier than was anticipated, thus showing the soundness of my rule not to contract. I believe the charge for the work done is very moderate under the circumstances.

Another client was left in no doubt about Deloitte's feelings:

I beg to thank the Directors for their kind expressions to me and for their check, which is not sufficient to remunerate me for the time employed in the matter, and unless some more satisfactory arrangement can be made for the payment of my services I must beg to withdraw from the Audit as I cannot afford to give my time without being paid and I being entirely dependent on my own exertions.

No satisfactory arrangement was made and Deloitte resigned from the position. Collection of accounts was slow and gave rise to much correspondence often of an acrimonious and threatening nature. By way of contrast, Deloitte could write in a more diplomatic frame of mind: 'I wish you would make me believe you have not forgotten me by sending me a remittance on account of my debt.' Occasionally the till ran dry and then the letters were of a more appealing nature. 'We are very short of money and shall therefore feel obliged by your forwarding us a check for £75 per account delivered at your earliest convenience.' Then, as now, the desirability of making clear to the client the scope of and responsibility for the services undertaken was fundamental, as the following letters testify:

I am sorry to hear that my Clerk made some mistake in the work he did for you, but I hope in this instance you will not blame me as I did

16

not interfere with him or have his work checked but simply at your request lent you a Clerk to assist you in taking stock etc., leaving him entirely under your control and direction.

and

In reply to your favour of yesterday we shall be happy to undertake the Audit of your Accounts. A confidential clerk would do the greater part of the labor, but only under the personal supervision of one of the firm: we never entrust any business—however small—entirely to clerks, but by a proper system we are enabled to diminish our labor and theirs also, and have at the same time absolute control over their work.

Great Western Railway

The Great Western Railway Company had been inaugurated in 1835 with a capital of £2,500,000. The outlook was apparently regarded as bright, for the opening sentence of the directors' report submitted at the Guildhall, Bristol, in August 1836, read: 'The Directors cheerfully fulfil the injunctions of the Act of Parliament in convening the proprietors for the first time within the walls of this city.' In 1838 the directors' report announced that eight daily trains each way (excepting on Sundays) were running between Paddington and Maidenhead: Sunday travelling —particularly to Maidenhead—was obviously frowned upon as wicked. The firm's long and close association with the Great Western Railway dates from 1849 when the accounts, audited by two lay auditors, were also signed 'W. W. Deloitte, Accountant'. The circumstances leading to Deloitte's appointment are of interest, reflecting a consciousness in those early days on the part of stockholders of the need for an intermediary between themselves and directors. A committee appointed in 1849 to consult with the board called 'special attention to the existing system of auditing the accounts' and urged upon the proprietors 'the expediency of taking this subject into their earliest consideration, with a view to the adoption of an efficient, independent system of audit'. As a result of the committee's inquiries the question of audit was extensively referred to in the directors' report on the accounts for the half-year to 31 December 1849 in the following terms:

The auditors have been assisted, for the first time, throughout a laborious examination of all the books, accounts and documents of the Company, by a public accountant, whom they appointed without previous communication with any individual connected with the Company. . . . They have, by their signatures, authenticated the accounts, and have expressed their general commendation of the system itself, and the mode in which it is worked. The auditors have stated to the Board their intention to attend the half-yearly meeting for the purpose of giving information, or expressing their opinions upon any matter of interest to the proprietors, and it is proposed by them that, for the future, the audit should be conducted more continuously, to which the Board has given its ready and unqualified consent. The Directors advert with satisfaction to those observations in the report of your Consultation Committee, which bear testimony on their part to the correctness of the accounts, a subject to which they had devoted their unremitting attention, quite irrespective of the audit itself. The matter so essentially involves the integrity of your affairs, and the fidelity of your officers, as to render such testimony of the highest value to the character of the undertaking.

Not content with dealing thus exhaustively and effectively with the situation as it then existed, surely a model conception of accountability by directors, the board showed what can only be regarded as remarkable prescience in suggesting that what they had attempted to do should be made compulsory by the legislature:

The directors must express an earnest desire . . . that some steps may be taken to secure the final adoption of an efficient and independent system of audit by a legislative measure during the present session. . . . Your Board will therefore content itself with reiterating the general opinion that the audit should be scrutinising, continuous and complete, conducted by persons wholly unconnected with, and independent of, directors and officers, but possessing the confidence of the proprietors. The auditors . . . should be assisted by a public accountant, their remuneration should be fully adequate to their labours, but fixed in amount. . . . They should be required to report their opinions freely and unreservedly, as well to the directors during the audit, as to the proprietors after it shall have been completed.

The auditors' duties and responsibilities were subsequently laid down by the Railway Companies Act 1867. A statutory form of railway accounts was prescribed in 1868 and it is believed that Deloitte, who by then had had considerable experience in railway audits, played a major part in designing the form and contents of such accounts since known as the double-account system: they were probably the first prescribed form of accounts in the modern sense. The diligence with which the auditors prosecuted their duties is evidenced by a statement in their report for 1868:

The whole of the expenditure for renewals of rolling stock, including many important improvements, has been charged to revenue. We have personally inspected some of the vehicles which have been reconstructed to replace others worn out, and are satisfied that the stock so substituted is of considerable increased value.

This is not the earliest instance of the physical inspection of stock by auditors, for we find Deloitte writing the following letter as early as 1856:

The stock of rails at Newport must be taken by me and you had better have an account taken by the various parties in charge of the rails along the line. The account will be taken as on the 30th June to correspond with your accounts but I need not see the rails until after that date.

The respective merits of equating expenditure on renewals or writing it off when it arose was the subject of a long dissertation in the board's report in 1842. The directors favoured the former method and adopted it until Isambard Kingdom Brunel, their famous engineer, expressed a contrary opinion.

Other railway clients

In the meanwhile Deloitte was extending his railway clientele to numerous companies associated with the Great Western and had also been appointed accountant to the auditors of the Lancashire & Yorkshire Railway: it was presumably primarily in connexion with this last-mentioned appointment that he formed a branch partnership in Manchester with James Halliday under the title of Deloitte & Halliday, although he may also have had in mind that Manchester at that period was rivalling London for commercial supremacy. The partnership was terminated amicably in 1877: Halliday later became managing director and subsequently chairman of the Manchester & Liverpool District Bank, now the District Bank.

Great Western Railway audit

From 1887 until his retirement in 1897 Deloitte acted as one of the joint auditors of the Great Western Railway and the audit committee of the board referred to this innovation in the following terms:

> After very careful consideration of the course to be pursued the committee have come to the conclusion that the election of Mr. Deloitte (who on behalf of his firm has been the acting accountant to the auditors for 38 years) would best serve the interests of the shareholders. Mr. Deloitte would appreciate the honour of the appointment and the shareholders will gain in the long experience and intimate knowledge of the company's affairs which his connection with the accounts will ensure. Moreover, though this is of comparatively minor importance, it is found that by this arrangement a pecuniary saving will be effected.

The dual capacity in which Deloitte personally and the firm acted gave rise to doubts in the mind of one shareholder as to the propriety of one individual, in effect, occupying positions in which there might be conflicting loyalties. This question is prominent in the report of the audit committee submitted to the shareholders two years later in 1889. After stating that they had discussed this question with the shareholder but had failed to convince him that his view was mistaken, the audit committee added:

> . . . in the recommendation they made in February 1887 that Mr. Deloitte should be elected one of the auditors, they were in no way influenced by the representation that his partnership was on the eve of termination and might not be renewed. Indeed they are of opinion that his responsibility to the proprietors is increased rather than otherwise by the position he holds of one of the auditors and at the same time partner in the firm employed by the auditors as their accountants. . . . They therefore recommend . . . that the appointment of the present auditors be continued involving (as such appointment does) their perfect right to employ such accountants as they together agree will best protect the proprietors' interests and efficiently perform the business of the audit.

The firm's records throw no light upon the statement that Deloitte's partnership was on the eve of termination in 1887. On his resignation as one of the auditors ten years later, when he retired from practice, there was a long hiatus before the appointment of another member of the firm as auditor in 1921, although the firm retained its appointment as accountants. It was in 1921 that the railways of the United Kingdom were grouped into four main systems in which the Great Western was the only line to retain its substantial identity and name. Other partners held office as auditor from then until 1948 when the railways were nationalized and the nostalgic memories of the old Great Western faded into the more prosaic 'British Railways—Western Region' with which the firm still retains its connexion as auditors. There can be no doubt that Deloitte's early association with the Great Western Railway was a major factor in laying the foundation of the firm's practice.

Redpath frauds

In 1856 there occurred one of the big sensations of the last century when the country was startled by the discovery of extensive frauds in the Registration Department of the Great Northern Railway involving sums said to be of not less magnitude than £150,000. The facts were reported in *The Times* of 16 November 1856:

Mr. Leopold Redpath was the registrar of shares and transfers of stock of the company and in that capacity had command over the whole of that part of its transactions. He had been in their service for nine or ten years but had not held the same office during the whole of that time. He was originally the chief clerk of Mr. Clarke, who at one period stood in the relationship of registrar to the company and on the retirement of that gentleman Mr. Redpath succeeded to the office, which he has just been compelled to relinquish under circumstances of such deep disgrace. He is about 45 years of age and married, but without children as we are informed, and having the appearance and address of a gentleman. Though in receipt of a salary not larger it is said than from £250 to £300 a year, he lived in a style of great elegance at 27 Chester Terrace, Regents Park, and he had also a country residence at Weybridge. His mode of life, so little in unison with the income he derived from the Great Northern Company, if known to the rest of the ministerial officers, though of itself calculated to awaken suspicion, would not appear to have had that effect, for, besides the office he held under the company, he had the reputation of being a successful speculator, which might account with some for the ease of his circumstances and lead to the inference that he only retained his position in the service of the railway company as another string to his bow. He had also a great character among all who knew him for acts of charity and benevolence, and not without reason it appears, for he is said to have spent large sums of money in this way from time to time. He was connected with several of the charitable institutions of the metropolis—among others, Christ's Hospital and the Royal Society of St. Anne, of both of which he is stated to be a Governor; and he was always ready to use his influence in favour of any deserving person desiring to avail himself of their benefits.

Only two cases of fraud against Mr. Redpath were brought under attention, but they are sufficient, with the light which Mr. Mowatt, the Secretary, threw upon the transactions, to show the mode in which Redpath operated. It is equally simple and audacious and furnishes a striking practical commentary upon the manner in which this part of the accounts of the company must have been audited.

Redpath it appears was himself a registered proprietor of stock of the Company. Transfer A. 8518 purported to be transfer from Mr. Henry Baker, of Upper Gower Street on 29th April 1853 of £500 A Stock in the Great Northern Railway for a consideration of £225 paid to him by

Mr. Leopold Redpath. Transfer 8519 purported to be a transfer in April 1853 by Mr. William Kitching of Wakefield to Mr. Leopold Redpath of £250 Consolidated A Stock. On referring to the register the stock was found in Mr. Redpath's name. Opposite the transfer number of 8518 and in the column of 'A Deferred' Stock was found £1,500. Opposite 8519 in the column of 'A Stock' was £1,250.

The pattern of Redpath's machinations is familiar to accountants; how often since have plausible rogues and swindlers followed the same technique of casting a cloak of respectability and apparent prosperity over their nefarious practices. It was in connexion with the Redpath defalcations that Deloitte's name first came prominently before the general public. He was invited by the auditors of the Great Northern Railway to act with them in investigating the frauds, and also to audit and report fully upon the accounts of the railway. The directors of the Great Western and of the Lancashire & Yorkshire railways also instructed him to examine their Stock Registers in order to allay anxiety on the part of their stockholders.

Staff problems

Deloitte became so overwhelmed with work that he had to refuse new business: in one letter he says: 'I am so busy that I am obliged to write to him declining the business, but introducing Mr. Wm. Turquand' (Mr. Turquand later became the first President of the Institute of Chartered Accountants in England and Wales in 1880). Staff problems became acute: he engaged many more clerks and we have it on the authority of the late Edward Allbeury, in whom no doubt his uncle confided at a later date, that 'the greatest difficulty was to find the money to pay the salaries of the large staff employed'. At that date

Deloitte's capital in the business was £800. He must have been a man of unbounded energy for in the midst of these heavy duties and preoccupations we find him taking considerable time and trouble to locate, admonish, discharge, and finally give another chance to a recalcitrant clerk of the name of Dodd. A glimpse, reminiscent of Dickens, is given in Deloitte's letter to the young man's mother:

I am extremely grieved to be obliged to report to you that I have been compelled to discharge your son from my office.

At the present time I am very busy, so much so that I shall require perhaps 20 or 30 Clerks, and on Saturday last as an excuse for his absence from business for three days the enclosed miserable scratch was handed to me by one of my Clerks which in consequence of his reputed bad conduct I did not believe. I therefore went myself twice on that date to Dolly's Hotel and the second time as late as 8 o'clock in the evening and found that he had been out all day altho' not at his business and had told the Lady at Dolly's that there was nothing for him to do as an excuse for his not going as usual to the office.

I have unfortunately had frequent occasion to complain of his irregularity and felt myself bound to make an example of him in justice to others as well as to enable me to enforce my regulations, and without paining you with a catalogue of his misconduct, I would strongly recommend you at once to remove him from London away from his associates and place him in some situation where he will sleep on the Premises and where he will have a severe master constantly at his elbow as I feel persuaded nothing else will save him from utter ruin.

His associates are not the Clerks in my Office, neither do I know who they are, but that they are of the most dangerous character I am perfectly certain from his conduct and his want of principle. I do hope that my having been compelled to take this step may result to his advantage by placing him in a position where he will not have the opportunity of turning night into day as I have reason to think has been the case.

I have had great patience and forbearance with him and if you knew all you would wonder how I could have kept him so long but I was in hopes after his last return from the country that he would keep his word and endeavour to establish a more favourable opinion in my mind.

Since writing the enclosed, Mrs. Dewhurst has been with me and at her most earnest solicitations I have determined to try him once more and hope you will write to him and urge him to be attentive to his duties and give up his bad companions but I still think if you can find employment for him where he will sleep in the home it would be better than his remaining with me.

Dodd repaid Deloitte ill for this reprieve for shortly afterwards we find a letter to the boy's mother reporting that her son had borrowed £3. 10s. from a client and given an I.O.U. for the amount signing it 'per pro W. W. D.' History does not relate what happened to the young man. Deloitte's concern that the behaviour of his staff should not tarnish the reputation of the firm is evidenced by a letter on 24 January 1856: 'I hope you will impress upon the minds of the clerks that I am anxious that the passes are not in any way abused and that they will conduct themselves with propriety while travelling, as they do not know who may be in the carriage and observe them.'

First partnership: Thomas Greenwood

It soon became apparent to Deloitte that he needed a partner to cope with the growing practice and to assist him particularly on the exacting railway investigations. He was fortunate in finding in Thomas Greenwood a partner whose experience eminently fitted him for this task. Greenwood had been chief of the Capital Office—presumably the Stock Registration Department—of the Great Western Railway, in which capacity he must have been known to Deloitte. He was said to be a singularly able and clear-headed accountant with a legal brain. Greenwood joined Deloitte in partnership on 11 March 1857, contributing £800 capital and the name of the firm became Deloitte & Greenwood. The letters written by the two partners, who got on well together, indicated that they were of a somewhat different temperament and outlook. Deloitte in his letters was occasionally abrupt with a decisive turn of mind: 'I received your letter of this date and think it perfect nonsense your wasting so much time'; whereas in Greenwood's correspondence the words were well chosen and the letters graced with the old world courtesy: 'reciprocating the kind feeling of your Board and holding them in highest esteem as I have done so long, I am gratified to learn their approval of my services, which be pleased to assure them shall be at all times at their command'. Much of the correspondence of the firm was written from Paddington Station where the partners appear to have spent a good deal of their time on the accounts of the Great Western Railway.

Disagreements on Redpath inquiry

That all did not go well with the Redpath inquiry is shown by a request from the auditors in May 1857 to suspend the investigation and adjustment of the Stock and Share Registers of the Company due, so far as one can judge, to disagreement on the question of fees and dissatisfaction with the rate of progress. There were threats of legal proceedings by the firm to recover their charges and an unhappy situation developed. In July 1857 the firm took the unusual course of ventilating their grievances in a long and somewhat involved letter to *The Railway Times* which presumably at that date had a wide circulation amongst railway shareholders. They wrote:

To the Editor of *The Railway Times*:
Sir,

Great Northern Frauds

In the official report of the proceedings of the meeting of the Great Northern proprietors held on the 8th instant, the Chairman in reference to our investigation of the stock registers appears to have stated:

'The expense as far as it has gone amounted to £4,700 and I believe Mr. Deloitte had not completed one-quarter of the work. I am reminded that he had investigated two stocks out of seven and it was not very clear that his work would be finished even by the end of the year.'

As the proprietors have thus been misinformed in the matter we think it our duty both to them and ourselves to correct the mis-statement and we request the favour of your permission to do so through the medium of your columns.

By the desire of the Auditors we sent them an account of our charges amounting to £2,000 to 31st March last, including cost of books, inclosed in a letter dated 21st April 1857 from which the following is an extract:

'In answer to your enquiry for an estimate of the time and cost in completion of our labours in the registration department, we beg to assure you that it is most difficult to form a correct notion of the time that may be occupied which regulates the expense: but after mature consideration our opinion is—In regard to time—that the preference stocks may be finished by the next meeting of the Proprietors, but that it would be unsafe to calculate upon the final completion of the original A and B Stocks before the end of the year: As to cost—that the expense of completing and reporting upon the work now in hand may ultimately amount to £5,000 but that with extended office accommodation and the progress of the investigation without

28

interruption of any unforeseen difficulty, it may be finished for considerably less than that sum, which we consider the maximum.'

The £2,000 expended and the £5,000 to be expended, together £7,000 included the whole cost of the investigation.

The auditors then represented it imperative that we should complete our labours by the coming meeting and pressed us exceedingly to do so and accommodation being provided in four additional rooms we were enabled to increase our staff and get the work so far under control that we told the Committee—Mr. Denison, a member of it being present—that we were working with a determination to finish by the meeting in August and hoped to do so.

Up to the date of our suspension, on account of the estimate of £5,000, we had expended about £2,000. It is true that two stocks only were completed but the expenditure had been upon the whole of them; £100 more would have finished another stock, and our experience and progress in the interim having confirmed the accuracy of our estimate, we are confident the balance (£2,500) would have covered our charges for the completion of the other four.

This in round numbers we distinctly stated in our concluding paragraph of our letter to the auditors of the 23rd May as follows:—

'We cannot refrain from expressing our regret that so large an expenditure of the Company should be rendered comparatively useless by the new Registers of the larger stocks remaining unfinished, especially as we consider the further sum of £3,000, being the balance of our estimate of April 21, would have enabled us to complete the whole work.'

We believe that our correspondence with the auditors including the letters from which the foregoing extracts are taken, has been before Mr. Denison, both as Chairman of the Board and as a member of the committee of investigation; yet his statement is that our further charges would have amounted to three times £4,700 or £14,100 and our total work to four times £4,700 or £18,800, the fact being that £2,600 only were required to finish, making in all £7,000 for which sum of £7,000 the Capital of the Company exceeding £8,000,000 received during 10 years with some 50,000 transfers would have been perfectly adjusted, exhibiting not only Redpath's frauds in detail but also the amount registered erroneously and recoverable, the calls unpaid and who owe them, the premiums received and discounts allowed on the issue of Stock, the unregistered Scrip held by Proprietors and the amount that properly should stand on the registers which had not been ascertained from the commencement of the undertaking.

We leave the Proprietors and the public to judge whether the matter was, or was not, fairly represented to the meeting.

DELOITTE & GREENWOOD

The inquiry came to a premature end: subsequent correspondence shows that the matter was ultimately settled, but the terms are not stated. The firm's profit and loss account for the half-year to 30 September 1857 showed that fees received amounted to only £536 and that a loss of £767 had been sustained making a heavy inroad upon the partners' capital of £1,600: the fees for the subsequent half-year (£3,237) were well in advance of the normal and it may be assumed they included a sum in settlement of the claim against the Great Northern Railway. The inquiries into the Share Registers of the Great Western and Lancashire & Yorkshire railways appear to have confirmed that they were free from irregularities.

Great Exhibition of 1851

In 1857 we find Deloitte writing to a correspondent who was seeking a position: 'I received your letter of 5th and can have no hesitation in expressing my opinion as to your being qualified to undertake the books of the Crystal Palace.' This was the monster palace of glass originally erected, with much foreboding on the part of the public, in Hyde Park to house the Great Exhibition of 1851, but which had since been re-erected at Sydenham where it stood defying its detractors until its destruction by fire in 1936. The exhibition, opened by the Queen, was designed (as was its successor, the Festival of Britain with less conspicuous success one hundred years later) to display the triumphs of British art and manufacture, and was one of the sensational events of the century. There were, however, gloomy prognostications of disaster and a correspondent wrote to *The Times* pointing out that although glass possessed certain advantages over other materials, it suffered the disability of being liable 'to fracture from the reverberations of sound. It appears that upon the arrival of the Queen at the Crystal Palace a Royal Salute is to be fired, and, if as is probable, the muzzles of the guns be presented towards the glass wall of the building . . . the result will be that the officiating gunner will carry off the honours of the day by creating a crash such as will render the loudest tones of the organ utterly insignificant.' A Commission was incorporated by Royal Charter to prepare a plan for applying the substantial surplus arising from the Exhibition towards advancing industrial education and the firm still audit the accounts of the Commission.

Early arbitrations

It is of interest to note that during these early years the services of both Deloitte and Greenwood were invoked as arbitrators.

Henry Dever

Henry Dever was admitted as the third partner in 1862 when the name of the firm became Deloitte, Greenwood & Dever.

John Gane, who was a colleague of Dever on the staff, said of him: 'By long training and high intelligence he was an accountant of the first rank and he brought to bear upon his work a mind remarkable for comprehensiveness combined with lucidity.' In later years one of his clerks described him as 'always very kind and fatherly'. The admission of Henry Dever to partnership established the practice in Deloittes, unbroken since that time, of recruiting partners in the London firm from those serving on the staff.

Retirement of Thomas Greenwood and his subsequent career

Unfortunately for the firm, Thomas Greenwood suffered a serious breakdown in health and retired in 1867: a document records that he was paid out £6,000 by Deloitte and Dever over a period of five years. However, Greenwood recovered, became a member of the London Stock Exchange, and founded the firm of Greenwood & Co. which became prominent in the railway market and in finding finance for railway development at home and abroad. He was a man of strong religious convictions and his views on the distribution of wealth appear to have been well in advance of his time. His grandson, who was named after his grandfather and was articled to Deloittes in the 1890's, has given us a brief sketch of his grandfather's religious and social outlook:

When a young man my grandfather made a resolve not to allow his wealth to exceed £40,000. Since by this time [*i.e. the early days of his stockbroking firm*] his wealth had increased to that maximum figure he retired from Greenwood & Co. My grandfather also resolved to give away 10% of his income, the percentage to increase if his income increased. The resolution to this effect is written on the front page of his private ledger. My grandfather then devoted himself to advising and helping Spurgeon, the famous preacher of the Metropolitan Tabernacle and was regarded as Spurgeon's right-hand man.

Thomas Greenwood took into his firm a young man from Deloittes' staff named Henderson who proved to be so efficient that he made him a partner: Henderson later became Sir Alexander Henderson, Bt., and subsequently Lord Faringdon, and was for many years chairman of the Great Central Railway. One of Henderson's colleagues on the staff was the late Baron Emile d'Erlanger who, as a very young man, was placed for about a year in Deloittes for the purpose of obtaining some accountancy experience. A colleague of Baron Emile recalls the Baron saying in later life, 'how much he benefited from the experience which he greatly enjoyed. Emile used to say that he spent an inordinate time in filling up bloody time slips.' When Baron Emile became the head of the well-known merchant bankers, Erlangers Ltd., his association with Deloittes was renewed. He was a director of many important undertakings including the company formed to construct a tunnel to France under the Straits of Dover, in which he had an ardent belief, and whose accounts from 1872 to 1882 were audited by the firm. Lord Faringdon's younger brother, H. W. Henderson, who was also with Deloittes for some years (he left in 1881 when his salary was £40 per annum), joined him at a later date as a partner in Greenwood, Henderson & Co. H. W. Henderson was for many years one of the trustees and managers of the London Stock Exchange. Greenwood & Co. was until recently recognizable in the title of the well-known firm of Cazenove Acroyds & Greenwood & Co., now shortened to Cazenove & Co., with whom their business was merged. Throughout the years in Deloittes there occur many instances of sons having followed their fathers to obtain experience as members of the staff, but to the family of Greenwood belongs the distinction of maintaining a connexion with the firm for four generations—one of the sons of Thomas Greenwood, three grandsons, and two great-grandsons have passed through the office.

A. R. Hollebone

We do not know when articles of clerkship were first introduced. John Gane has said that they were not in fashion in 1857. A. R. Hollebone was probably the firm's first articled clerk, for under a deed dated 24 July 1861, which has been preserved, Deloitte undertook to teach and instruct him for a period of five years in the business, practice, profession, or employment of an accountant for the somewhat odd and surprisingly high premium at that time of £499. A fee of £525 was charged by the firm for articles until 1945 when acceptance of premiums was discontinued as being out of accord with modern tendencies. There is a clause in Hollebone's articles reminiscent of the old apprenticeships in the time when the City Guilds flourished:

And that the said William Joshua Hollebone his executors and administrators shall and will from time to time, and at all times during the said term of five years if the said Alfred Richard Hollebone shall so long continue to serve the said William Welch Deloitte at his and their proper costs and charges find and provide the said Alfred Richard Hollebone with good and sufficient board and lodging and with all and all manner of necessary and becoming apparel and medicine and medical attendances in case of sickness—except that during such times as the said Alfred Richard Hollebone shall be absent from London on the business of the said William Welch Deloitte he the said William Welch Deloitte shall find and provide the said Alfred Richard Hollebone with good and sufficient board and lodging and pay his travelling expenses.

Since Hollebone's day thirteen partners have served their articles with the firm. Hollebone was only 16 years of age when the articles were signed and his promotion to partnership in 1867 at the age of 22 after only six years' practical experience must surely constitute a record for Deloittes. The name of the firm became Deloitte, Dever, Hollebone & Co. Until 1888 the names of all members of the firm were included in the style of the firm and the addition of '& Co.' was doubtless made in anticipation of the introduction of further partners. After six years Hollebone resigned and joined the stockbroking firm of Hollebone Brothers & Trench, of which he became the senior partner, and where, according to his son, 'he introduced a marvellous system of book-keeping; if he walked round the office glancing at the books and there happened to be a slight error he always spotted it'. He must indeed have possessed an eagle eye! He was said to be a man of sport and hunted with The Old Surrey, but although of robust appearance he was not constitutionally strong and only survived his retirement for a few years. The firm of Hollebone Brothers & Trench was merged some years ago with the well-known firm of J. & A. Scrimgeour. It is a matter of gratification to Deloittes, after having contributed two former partners as prominent members of the House, that the firm has for many years acted as auditors of the London Stock Exchange.

In 1869 another member of the staff was promoted to partnership status who was destined until his retirement in 1902 to exercise a major influence on the growth and fortunes of the firm. John George Griffiths has himself recorded his first impressions of Deloittes:

I well recollect my first introduction to 4, Lothbury, in the early spring of 1865, when I arrived there, a disappointed lad, in the belief that no career would ever open itself for me now that I had been obliged to give up the commission in the Army [*he had resigned for frail health*] to which I had only just been appointed. I knew nothing of the City, and I had no friend there except my cousin, Alfred Hollebone, then an articled clerk to Mr. Deloitte.

A short time, however, in the company of a few clerks who then formed the staff of Messrs. Deloitte, Greenwood & Dever removed much of my depression, and my good friend, Gane, then the senior clerk, and other good fellows, soon made it clear to me that there was a prospect there for a man who meant work; so I persuaded my father to apply the greater part of the price of my commission to the cost of my Articles to Mr. Greenwood, and I was launched on a new career with, I am happy now to think, far better prospects than the Army could have offered me.

Things were different at 4, Lothbury in those days to what they ultimately became: there were periods when even the seven or eight clerks in the office were more than enough for the amount of work available; and there was an eager rush for any that fell to be done. I had reason to be grateful to John Gane for then giving me my first insight into the mysteries of accounts, and enabling me to qualify, to some extent, for the work I had to do.

Thus, John Griffiths, albeit reluctantly, reversed the roles of Sir Walter Scott's nephew who became a soldier after he had con-

The Mansion House
(The official residence of the Lord Mayor of London)

sidered and rejected the advice of his uncle 45 years earlier in 1820: 'If my nephew is steady, cautious, fond of a sedentary life and quiet pursuits and at the same time proficient in arithmetic and with the disposition towards the prosecution of its highest branch, he can not follow a better line than that of an accountant.' John Gane, a lifelong friend of John Griffiths, has concisely summed up the chief characteristics which contributed to his highly successful career: 'not only is he one of the best accountants who ever grappled with figures, but he is the fortunate possessor of those other all-round qualities which go to make up a complete business man'. And a late, much respected, member of the staff who was closely associated with John Griffiths towards the end of the nineteenth century recorded this appreciation of him: 'For him and his abilities I always had the greatest admiration. Although his discipline was rather on the stern side, he was always just and one was eager to please him.' The writer, who in his early days took down Mr. Griffiths's letters, may have been casting his mind back to the late evenings he spent at the office where it was the habit of Mr. Griffiths to return in the late afternoon and dictate until he felt it was time to go home for dinner.

The premium on John Griffiths's articles in March 1865 was £315, apparently for a reduced period of three years. There were then no accountants' organizations or examinations and presumably principals determined the length and conditions of service under articles. In 1866 Griffiths received a salary of £50, raised to £100 in 1867. As the salaries in 1866 of the firm's managing clerks of some years standing ranged between £80 and £160, the services of Griffiths were highly rated even in his probationary years. It was a remarkable achievement on Griffiths's part to attain partnership status at the early age of 24 with only four years' practical experience. The name of the firm was again changed to Deloitte, Dever, Hollebone & Griffiths, but on Hollebone's retirement four years later it became, and remained for thirty-two years, Deloitte, Dever, Griffiths & Co., although in that period six additional partners were admitted.

The early years of Griffiths's service with the firm saw the sensational failure of the well-known banking house of Overend Gurney & Co. on Thursday, 10 May 1866, with £5 m. liabilities, and the following day was long to be remembered in the City of London as Black Friday. It was followed by many failures of banks, financial and mercantile houses, no doubt providing much insolvency work for accountants. Apart from the temporary setback of remarkably short duration caused by the Franco-German war in 1870 the trade of the country expanded rapidly, helped by the opening in 1869 of the Suez Canal: exports of capital and capital goods were at their highest in 1871–3, aided by immense railway building activity overseas, particularly in the United States, largely financed by the United Kingdom. Sir John Clapham in his *History of the Bank of England* says: 'The years from 1866 to 1873, as seen from any public standpoint, by statesmen or banker, merchant or industrialist, look like a gigantic hinge on which the history of the later nineteenth century turns.' Deloittes were fortunate in finding in John George Griffiths a partner whose initiative, ability, and capacity kept pace with the march of events during and after that eventful period.

John Griffiths has left a brief record of a few important inquiries conducted by the firm in the late 1860's, in a speech which he made in 1911:

The purchase by the Government of the Inland Telegraphs led to the employment of Deloitte & Company in 1868 and 1869 to assist in the protection of the interests of shareholders, and I was entrusted with the greater part of this work under the instructions of my dear friend, Henry Dever: it is interesting to recollect that my most useful and earnest assistant in this work was the brilliant financier, Sir Alexander Henderson, then a very young man.

Since March 31st, 1869, when I joined the firm as a partner with a very limited interest in the profits, very many events of importance to me have occurred, with which I need not trouble you. I may, however, mention the inquiries into Egyptian financial affairs by Mr. Stephen Cave and Mr. Goschen in the days of the Khedive Ismail, before the English occupation, when the firm was concerned on behalf of the Egyptian Government, and when their report on the principles of the consolidation of the Egyptian Bonded Debt was referred to, with respect, in the House of Commons.

During the many years from March 1869 to September 1902, when I retired from the firm, its position in the estimation of the public and the profession matured and was consolidated: but the feature of our progress which most often occurs to my mind as the most important element of our success is the earnest co-operation and sympathy we received from a succession of devoted and talented men who took service with us. I cannot exaggerate this. These men and many like them, were keen for the success of the firm, and they took real pleasure in the credit which accrued to the firm for work which we could not possibly have performed without their able and strenuous assistance.

This loyalty has been one of the main characteristics of the staff at 4, Lothbury: there has always been a real pride in the firm on the part of the clerks, and a determination to give their best work in promoting the firm's interests.

I have reason to believe that this quality still exists, and I hope and believe it is engendered by a feeling of true comradeship and mutual confidence and esteem between the members of the firm and the staff.

Telephone investigation

It also appears that the firm was engaged on the investigation of the accounts of several telephone companies (National Telephone Company, United Telephone Company, and the Lancashire & Cheshire Telephone Company) with a view to a merger of their interests. This was no doubt an initial stage in the formation of the National Telephone Company which subsequently operated, with a few local exceptions, the telephone system in the United Kingdom. (The first reference to the use of the telephone in the office—No. 196—occurs in a letter written in February 1888, and the annual rental at that time was £20.) Some years later, in 1912, the National Telephone Company was taken over by the Post Office. In fixing the consideration a major factor was the ascertainment of the depreciation of plant and installations to be deducted in arriving at the maintainable profits of the undertaking. Many of the leading accountants, including a partner in the firm, gave evidence on this difficult and highly technical question, although at that time the witnesses did not have to consider the effect of inflation on replacement values which looms so large today.

London, Chatham & Dover Railway

We find the firm in 1866 undertaking more work in the railway world, this time an investigation, jointly with another firm, into what John Griffiths called 'the intricate affairs' of the London, Chatham & Dover Railway, absorbed many years ago into the old London & South Western Railway. Those still among us of a dwindling generation will remember the roars of laughter which greeted the then popular name for that line—the London, Smashem and Turnover—when mentioned, as it frequently was, as a topical joke in the Old Victorian music halls: Mr. Macqueen-Pope in his entertaining book, *Twenty Shillings in the Pound*, relates how the comedian would 'tell tales of passengers getting out and picking flowers whilst the train moved slowly along and of young boys who became bearded patriarchs before the journey's end'.

Cable companies

About this time also began the firm's long and close association with the cable companies. After financial and physical frustrations which would have led less adventurous men to abandon the project, the first Anglo-American cable was successfully laid and operated in 1866; the leading spirit was Cyrus W. Field, a shrewd and able American man of business and one of the pioneers of submarine telegraphy. With Cyrus Field was associated the firm's old clients, the Telegraph Construction & Maintenance Co. Ltd., a company merging the interests of Glass, Elliott & Co., and the Gutta Percha Company, which manufactured the cable and participated in the finance, and whose chairman was John Pender. There was only one ship big enough to lay the cable, the famous *Great Eastern*, a leviathan for those days of 22,500 tons, chartered by the Telegraph Construction & Maintenance Co. Ltd. for the purpose. Sir Daniel Gooch, chairman of the Great Western Railway, was also chairman of the company owning the *Great Eastern* steamship: no information is now available of the great fraud in that company which the firm is said to have investigated and unravelled. The early 1870's saw the formation of many other cable companies, with which the name of Sir John Pender will always be associated, amongst them being the Eastern Telegraph Co. Ltd. (by which company Cyrus W. Field was honoured by being appointed an Extraordinary Director), the Western Telegraph Co. Ltd. (originally named the Brazilian Submarine Telegraph Co. Ltd.), the West India & Panama Telegraph Co. Ltd., and the Eastern Extension Australia & China Telegraph Co. Ltd. The firm was appointed auditors of all these companies, the head offices of which were located for many years in Electra House, Moorgate Street, and it was the custom in later years for newly arrived articled clerks to spend some months there to master the rudiments of accountancy and auditing. One articled clerk created a sensation by arriving there in a four-in-hand driven by a retainer complete with top hat and cockade, a proceeding which was considered inappropriate by his seniors and was not repeated.

An early report to the directors of West India & Panama Cable Co. Ltd. showed that the system of accounting was not all that it should be:

We have thoroughly examined the accounts of the company for the year to 30 September 1873 and have found it necessary to make numerous alterations therein introducing all the ascertained and undisputed liabilities of the company at that date. We may state that it is quite impossible to prepare an accurate statement of affairs of this company so soon after the close of the financial year as November 7th, the date on which the accounts were signed: it being necessary to introduce estimated figures which have in most cases proved erroneous as the accounts from abroad cannot be properly examined and entered into the books within five weeks of leaving the stations.

The directors of one of the other companies in the group evidently consulted the firm and fortified themselves against a similar situation by passing the following minute:

A letter was read from Messrs. Deloitte, Dever & Co. offering to superintend the keeping of the books of the Company. It was resolved that the Board do avail itself of the services of Messrs. Deloitte, Dever & Co. on the terms stated.

The inauguration of cables had a marked effect upon the speed of transactions in the financial centres of the world, as evidenced by the following extract from the report in 1874 of the Exchange Telegraph Co. Ltd.:

Arrangements have been made to supply subscribers at certain periods during the day with American and Continental stock Exchange prices: the New York and Paris services have been some time in operation and Berlin, Vienna, Constantinople etc. will soon be added to the list. The improvements recently effected in the Company's instruments, by which the speed is more than doubled and a much greater security insured, admit of these services being given over them without prejudice to local matter.

The present chairman of the Exchange Telegraph Co. Ltd., Wm. C. Stevens, is one of many former members of the staff who have entered the service of clients upon whose audit they had been engaged.

Before the advent of cable and telegraph services pigeon post had been the means by which news was rapidly passed between important centres. Among the pioneers of the news-distributing agencies was Paul Julius Reuter who established a carrier pigeon service on the Continent in 1844 for the transmission of stock market prices between commercial centres. That this method of communication still had its uses was demonstrated nearly a century later when during the invasion of Normandy by the Allied Forces in 1944 the correspondents of Reuters Ltd., who are clients of the firm, sent their dispatches from Normandy to England by pigeon post.

South American Railways

The thirty years between 1860 and 1890 saw the almost continuous construction of railways in overseas countries, particularly in South and Central America, and this activity aided by a steady stream of immigrants from Europe did more than almost anything else to develop that continent. The firm numbered amongst its clients the principal main lines with their subsidiary branch companies in the Argentine and many railways in Brazil, Bolivia, Chile, Colombia, Cuba, Mexico, Paraguay, Uruguay, and Venezuela. John Griffiths was responsible for organizing the accounts of the English railway companies in the Argentine on a gold basis.

Information in old letter books 1887–8

Unfortunately only three letter books of the nineteenth century in addition to the letter book of 1854–8 have escaped destruction, those covering the period from July 1887 to October 1888. Nearly all the letters are in the partners' handwriting and the press copies are remarkably distinct: most of the letters by far were written in the clear and legible hand of John Griffiths,

44

who seems to have had a tremendous capacity for work. We see him keeping a close watch on the movements of the staff and the detailed work on which they were engaged, and travelling extensively in the country to discuss accounts and keep in touch with clients. His clerk has recorded: 'I remember Sir George Elliott for whom, whenever he was coming to the office to see Mr. Griffiths, I had to go out and buy some fresh ground snuff.' John Griffiths did not apparently possess the same facility of speaking in public as he did in expressing himself in writing: 'It is my intention to attend your General Meeting and although I hate speaking in public I will endeavour to give the office the good character it deserves.' His services were in great demand and his advice much sought: he took a keen interest in professional matters and in questions of national moment which brought him into contact with many well-known political and other figures of the day. The letters show that there was a considerable influx of new business and John Griffiths appears to have handled the bulk of it: Deloitte was approaching his seventieth year and although he was dealing with matters of office routine he seems to have been content to leave most of the work to his two partners, Henry Dever and John Griffiths, and to the chief clerk George Cloutte who had joined the staff in 1869 and was admitted to partnership in 1889. Cloutte was described by one who knew him intimately as 'the incarnation of a highly trained hard working accountant'. The letters give a valuable insight into the conduct of the business and the characteristics of the partners. They do not throw much light upon the professional standards and quality of the firm's work or reveal the highlights of the practice, and in the absence of current report books and audit and other papers recourse has been had to such other contemporary documents as are available, and to clients to whom the firm is grateful for their help in piecing together some of the more important events and occasions in the earlier period of the firm's existence.

London & River Plate Bank fraud

We find John Griffiths going to Paris each half-year on the audit of the London & River Plate Bank, and there is a letter from Deloitte to the bank making an appointment for the examination of the bank's securities in London. Edward Allbeury has described a sensational discovery by Mr. Deloitte, which was talked about for many years in the office but has been almost forgotten in the passage of time. He says:

In the early eighties I was behind the scenes in the London & River Plate Bank affair in which a large amount was involved. I had been engaged on the London audit with a Mr. Walter Lean, who was Mr. Deloitte's right-hand man (the most noteworthy feature about this man was that he was a Quaker and the father of twelve children living at that time). Mr. Deloitte always made it a point to examine the bank's securities himself with Lean's assistance. It seems that the Manager brought in part of the securities (mostly bearer bonds) and when these had been examined he started to take them away but Mr. Deloitte said they were to be left till all the securities had been examined. He left the room and after some time Mr. Deloitte asked for him and was told he had gone out. The security clerk then brought the remainder and it was found according to the list that a large number were missing amounting to many thousand pounds. It afterwards transpired that if he (the Manager) could have taken the first lot of securities from the room he could have rushed them to his bankers and exchanged them for others which they held as security for a very large sum. A warrant was taken out

46

the next day and inquiries were made for three or four days when to the surprise of Scotland Yard he presented himself there. It seems he went to Paris on the evening of the examination but when he got there he found he had only a few pounds in his pocket so he decided to return and give himself up; he travelled all the way to Scotland Yard without being recognised. He got several years penal servitude. I happened to be in the office when I saw Mr. Deloitte coming back from the examination supported by Mr. Lean and looking very white and ill: we managed to get him some brandy.

Business in the United States

Early in March 1888 John Griffiths sailed from Queenstown for New York at the request of Alexander Henderson to conduct an inquiry into a railroad proposition: he stayed at Brevoort House and was absent about a month, during which time the office was punctilious in keeping him informed by cable of the state of affairs at 4, Lothbury. About this time the firm had been carrying on numerous investigations into businesses in New York, Boston, Brooklyn, Chicago, Denver, Kentucky, Minneapolis, and Philadelphia. Whilst on an investigation leading to a brewery amalgamation John Griffiths's younger brother, Percival Davis Griffiths, who had joined the staff in 1880, suggested he should remain in New York and practise on his own account. Incidentally, some past and present members of the firm's staff who can recall their own shortcomings may read with sympathy a cable sent to P. D. Griffiths in New York by his brother:

You must report fully and positively, leave nothing to my discretion as I cannot judge here. Your abbreviated sentences are barely comprehensible especially the middle of last message. Please avoid them.

47

Nothing further appears about the suggestion made by P. D. Griffiths, but the partners must have been impressed with the amount of business being offered in the United States. In 1890 a branch office was opened in Wall Street with Edward Adams and P. D. Griffiths as Branch Managers: Adams subsequently became resident partner. This was the first of the firm's overseas offices. One of the first clients of New York Office was a tobacco firm, still well known, to whom a certificate was given in connexion with the conversion of the business into a company. Branches were also opened about this time in Chicago and Buenos Aires, but they appeared in the noteheading of London Office only for a very brief period. Nothing is known about their activities apart from the Buenos Aires Office having been under the management of a former member of the London staff, who subsequently became Chief Accountant to clients of the firm and was said to possess an imaginative and lurid vocabulary equal to any situation. Branches of New York Office were opened in later years at Cincinnati (1905), Chicago (1912), Montreal (1912), Boston (1930), and Los Angeles(1945). Agency arrangements for the Pacific Coast were entered into with Maclaren Goode & Co. of San Francisco, now merged in the firm of Haskins & Sells with whom Deloittes subsequently formed a close association. Agency arrangements for Western Canada were made with Helliwell, Maclachlan & Co. of Vancouver.

Business in South Africa, Canada, and Europe

The firm's connexions in other places abroad had been increasing. Edward Adams had spent several months in South

Africa in 1888 at Barberton (in connexion with the famous Sheba Gold Mines), Kimberley (on the Victoria Diamond Company of de Beer), and Cape Town. John Griffiths wrote to him: 'I shall be very glad to see you back here again. I am almost obliged to conceal the fact that you are in Africa for fear of getting more work for you to do there.' A promising young member of the staff, by name William Plender, had been in Canada in 1887 to investigate a case of embezzlement and he remained there and in the United States for nine months. This must have been the trip about which Lord Plender, as he afterwards became, used to relate an amusing incident. Travelling from Montreal to New York, and being unfamiliar with American habits, he put his boots out in the corridor to be cleaned. The next morning they had disappeared and he had to walk from the railway station to a cab in his socks. Many years later Lord Plender recalled his travels on behalf of the firm about this time:

On my returning to London the continental work was allotted to me, and on the firm's business I visited practically every country in Europe. It was a happy experience for a young man not only in gaining knowledge of continental business matters, but in giving him the opportunity to become acquainted with life in centres like Paris, Madrid, Seville, Rome, Vienna in the days of the Hapsburgs, Berlin, Brussels, Antwerp, Constantinople, Prague (where clashes took place on certain feast days between the Czechs and Germans, leading often to blows and sometimes worse, and I frequently saw the Austrian Archduke driving an English dogcart with a small tiger behind him, whilst he was stationed with his regiment in that city), St. Petersburg and Moscow (when the Tsar was on the throne) and the towns on the Baltic. I also had opportunities when in those cities of seeing the picture galleries, museums and historic buildings which I could not have done in the limited holidays of two or three weeks a year.

I cannot say I had any very exciting experiences on my business trips though a few small—perhaps trivial—incidents remain in my memory, some of which I might mention. I never kept a diary.

I remember being in a café in Madrid with a Spanish friend connected with an electrical undertaking owned by an English company whose affairs I was sent to examine, and the large room where we sat for supper one evening was partitioned off like the old family pews in some village churches, with a table in the centre, and the waiter brought refreshments to us there. My friend said that the people in the next compartment were getting very excited in a discussion about religion and the monarchy, and my friend said 'It will not be long before some knives are used or shots are fired, and as soon as I give you a knock, get down under the seats and remain there.' We had not been hidden in that way more than a few minutes when shots rang out; people were injured and carried out, but we remained untouched.

In the same city we were dining one evening with a well-known Englishman who had married a Spanish lady. He was a most interesting man, but of violent temper, and when the butler brought round the leg of mutton for our host to carve, it was found to be under-done, and our host lost his temper, threw the leg of mutton out of the window behind him and it fell in the street, so that there was no mutton for us for that night's dinner. His wife was overcome by her husband's behaviour, and left the table in a temper.

On one occasion in the Ural Mountains where I was engaged on investigations into the oil industry, an English friend asked me if I would care to go with him to visit the governor of a province with a view to trying to get information of a somewhat confidential nature relating to the holding of certain oil-bearing lands which my friend wanted to have knowledge of. The governor received us in quite a friendly way, and when my friend made his request he was told it was quite impossible to give him the information as the records were of a secret nature. There was, resting on the governor's table, a silk hat which looked as if it had just been ironed by Lincoln Bennett & Co. The governor, after having told us that the information was not available, left his desk and walked over to a large window at the end of the room overlooking the garden and lit a cigarette. Whilst his back was turned, my friend took out of his pocket a few 1,000 rouble notes, rustled them and dropped them in the hat. The governor knew what had happened. After a short interval he returned from the window, walked to his seat and looked down inside his hat and saw something there which interested him. He thereupon said that it was a pity my friend had come so long a distance without getting what he set out for, so he gave him a card of introduction to the Custodian of the Records, and they were immediately placed at my friend's disposal and he got the facts which he wanted.

The only occasion on which I was offered a bribe was in a city in the Eastern part of the Continent. I had with me an assistant to conduct an investigation into the accounts of a number of breweries. The books at one brewery were very badly kept, and my colleague and I worked well into the night for a week or two to see if we could make something out of what was practically chaos. We did not succeed in getting any reliable figures but an approximation of the facts was ascertained which could not, however, be certified as correct. When we were leaving the railway station for home the intermediary between the vendors of the under-taking and a finance syndicate in London that was to undertake the pro-motion of a proposed company, said to me that he never expected there would be such trouble in connection with the accounts and that it could not have been foreseen when the fee of my firm was fixed to make the inquiry, and he said that he would like to reward me for the extra trouble I had voluntarily taken and offered me a little bag which con-tained 100 sovereigns. It was a bribe, and I refused it, and told him that if he wanted to remunerate my principals he could send the money direct to London. It never came, and the company when formed proved a failure. Had I yielded to temptation my career might have been not merely jeopardized but completely broken.

I recall a visit I paid to Northern France to make investigation of a number of distilleries in conjunction with another London firm of chartered accountants. None of the businesses was particularly flourish-ing with one exception, and out of curiosity I thought I would like to

51

see the distillery in which success had been achieved far beyond that of any of the other distilleries. I made several suggestions as to visiting the premises in question, and whilst promises were made that I could go, days passed without any definite appointment being made, and I said that unless I could go I should have to report the fact. I was then taken there, and as we approached the town I looked out for a large building and chimneys, but I saw nothing of the sort and was taken to some small buildings which had the appearance of stables. I showed some surprise, and was told that manufacturing was on a comparatively small scale, although they appeared to have a large stock of well-known brands, such as Chartreuse, Benedictine, etc. with the labels on the bottles as if they had come direct from the famous monasteries where such liqueurs were made. My surprise was somewhat noticeable and I was told that they had a printing press there and that they forged the labels themselves and these were put on the bottles which had very inferior contents. They said they had enormous sales for them at good prices in low-class cafés in Paris and Marseilles and such-like places. I need hardly tell you that the proposed company never materialised and the scheme was dropped.

One pleasing incident in connection with the visit was that in one town, Douai by name, where the owner of a distillery lived in a charming old house and was overwhelmingly hospitable to us in the evenings. We often went to dinner with him and his family and after an excellent meal with some good wine, we English people were asked to walk round the table singing English songs and we were followed by members of his own large family of boys and girls who sang French songs. They were very happy, if somewhat hilarious, evenings.

When I was in St. Petersburg I was invited with other Englishmen out to dinner occasionally by Russian friends. Before going into the dining-room we passed through a small ante-room where caviare sandwiches were served plentifully, with an abundance of vodka, which we found to be a particularly strong stimulant. We were pressed to take more than was good for us, and sometimes we yielded and before dinner was over, which was on a gigantic scale, we were in a somewhat dazed condition much to our Russian friends delight, as it showed that the English had fully appreciated their hospitality.

In the Caucasus, life was cheap some fifty or sixty years ago. There was said to be a tariff for getting rid of undesirable residents or visitors, the highest price being for an Englishman's removal. I saw a murder of a Turk in the streets of Batum and on the night train I travelled by between Batum and Baku I heard in the morning on arriving at Baku that a French dressmaker had been murdered by bandits who had boarded the train and got away. None of the officials seemed much concerned.

During World War II the Lofoten Islands off the northern coast of Norway figured for a brief period in the fighting and it is strange to read that in 1888 the firm had been engaged in making a valuation of the goodwill of a business carried on in those islands. It is a far cry from the icy north to read of a review made by the firm about the same time of the revenues derived from the hereditary estates of the Maharajah of Bettiah.

Growth of business

The firm's staff increased gradually from thirty in 1882 to sixty-six in 1891 and eighty in 1900, and in the earlier years the partners were in some danger of being overwhelmed with work beyond their capacity to handle. We read: 'We are particularly pressed in all directions but if Mr. Cloutte can get clear he will be with you on Thursday'. Work flowed in from the Midlands, particularly in North Staffordshire, where a resident staff was kept to work on the numerous colliery, ironworks, and pottery audits. George Cloutte had charge of these for many years and paid frequent visits there. Another letter can hardly have created a good impression on the recipient: 'I am sorry I cannot make any other appointment than that I have suggested. The fact is I am so much engaged that I am not disposed to take up any new business except it is of a character neither of anxiety nor too much trouble.' And the following conclusion to a report to old and valued clients was, to say the least, lacking in tact: 'We regret exceedingly that these reports have occupied so much more time than we anticipated which has arisen partly from the necessity of the subject requiring the personal attention of Mr. Deloitte who is liable to constant interruptions by many other important matters in his hands.' There is no clue to the nature of an inquiry from a Mr. H. Deloitte of Sydney, N.S.W.—presumably a nephew—to which our Mr. Deloitte replied somewhat coldly: 'Dear Sir, We received your favour of the 10th Feb. and regret we cannot undertake the matter to which you refer.'

Institute of Chartered Accountants in England and Wales

The Institute of Chartered Accountants in England and Wales was incorporated by Royal Charter in 1880. W. W. Deloitte, Henry Dever, and John Griffiths became foundation members with Deloitte and Griffiths as original members of the council. Since then there has always been one partner, and sometimes two, on the Institute council. Apart from five partners in the firm who have since filled the office of president, four former members of the staff, who left to set up in practice, have reached the chair: Joseph John Saffery (1889–91)[1] who laid the foundation stone of the Institute in Moorgate Place, John Gane (1905–6),[1] Richard Henry March (1927–8),[1] and Clare Smith (1932–3).[1]

[1] Partners in the firms of (1) Saffery, Sons & Co., (2) Gane, Jackson, Jefferys & Freeman, (3) R. H. March, Son & Co., and (4) Hudson, Smith, Briggs & Co.

The days had long passed when the early struggle for business was carried on without regard to professional etiquette and courtesy and the emergence of an organized profession demanded a high degree of independence and integrity. It is pleasing to note the courtesies observed by the firm in avoiding anything in the nature of poaching or improper competition:

I am very sorry I did not know that you were likely to be concerned for the Bank before I was put forward [*as auditor*] as I should have had much pleasure in stepping aside at the last meeting.

and

In reply to your observations as to my having addressed your clients direct you will kindly excuse me for correcting you in the assumption that I had any knowledge of your connection with the business: in which case only, I would submit, could I be accused of not acting in accordance with the usual practice.

There is also a letter in which the firm refused to quote a fee for an audit in competition with another firm, but they added that if desired they would be willing to act as joint auditors. The desire to avoid conflicting interests or offence to the susceptibilities of others is shown in the following letter:

I have submitted the draft Prospectus of the Anglo Chilian Nitrate and Railway Co. Ltd. to my senior partner Mr. Deloitte and he agrees with me in saying that he sees no reason from our own point of view why we should not act as auditors to the company as kindly suggested by Messrs. Bircham and Company. At the same time we shall be obliged if you will kindly not put our name in the Prospectus unless your Chairman and other Directors whom you would usually consult are informed of our being auditors to the Nitrate Railways Company and, further, we should be very much obliged to you if, should it be the opinion of those gentlemen or yourself that our acting for both companies would have the slightest detrimental effect or lead to any questions of a disagreeable character, you will remove our name and appoint some other firm in our stead.

In another letter it is stated: 'I regret that neither Mr. Dever nor I can see our way to joining the Board.' It has been the policy of the firm from the first that partners should not accept office as directors of companies.

Metropolitan Life Assurance Society

It is rare nowadays to find a company which, by its articles, precludes the appointment of an auditor who acts for another company carrying on a similar class of business. John Griffiths endeavoured to free himself from such a restriction in a letter to the Metropolitan Life Assurance Society:

Referring to our interview this morning I write to ask you to be kind enough to inform me at your earliest convenience whether there is any reason why my firm should not act as auditors to a Life Insurance Society other than your own, notwithstanding the limitation which prevents me individually being the auditor for any other company and I shall be much obliged if you will let me have your views at the earliest possible moment.

As I have previously explained to you, the limitation in the Trust Deed of the Society is extremely inconvenient and may eventually oblige me to retire from the position of auditor to your Society as I cannot be expected, I think, in my professional position, to give up the opportunity of undertaking remunerative business in consequence of my connection with the Society.

I am, however, very desirous of continuing to act as your auditor and I think it is not unreasonable to ask that at the earliest opportunity the

Trust Deed be altered so as to enable me to act in my professional position as auditor to other Societies or Companies as well as your own.

You can, I am sure, readily believe me to be incapable of conveying any facts relating to your Society to the officials of any other company and I can imagine no other reason which would account for the restriction at present existing.

Prudential Assurance Co. Ltd.

His plea was apparently unsuccessful and he appears to have resigned and so prepared the way for the firm's subsequent connexion with other life offices. The immediate cause of John Griffiths's letter appears to have been an invitation to act from the Prudential Assurance Co. Ltd., for we find a paragraph in the directors' report for 1889 which says:

The large and rapidly increasing amount of the Funds of the Company has led the Directors to the determination that in future the Balance Sheet shall be subjected to an independent professional audit. For this purpose they engaged the services of Messrs. Deloitte, Dever, Griffiths & Co. whose certificate is appended to the Accounts. They feel sure that this course will meet with the approval of the Shareholders, and will increase public confidence in the stability of the Company.

The Prudential Assurance Company was founded in 1848 with a capital of £100,000. Its assets at the date of the firm's appointment amounted to nearly £11 m.: at 31 December 1956 they totalled over £850 m. It is not often that one finds clergymen undertaking the duties of auditors of public companies, but when the firm first became associated with the Prudential the Rev. T. H. Cole was an additional auditor.

John Griffiths writes in 1888: 'I have not seen the proposals of the Trust Company you mention. A good many are I believe in contemplation as those already formed have been so successful.' At that time there was immense activity in the formation of investment trusts and the firm secured a good share of the work. There is correspondence between Mr. Griffiths and Mr. Verner whose name was to figure prominently in the law case so well known to articled clerks as *Verner* v. *General & Commercial Trust.* There are still a fair number who can recall a veteran member of the staff, H. W. Powell (1887–1937), known as the Investment Trust King, who spent a large part of his time on the audits and security examinations of the Trusts. No one ever saw him dressed otherwise than in a frock coat and top hat, though he occasionally sported a red tie.

Company prospectuses

The firm was concerned in many capital issues. It liked to know the type of directors with whom it was to be associated:

On my return from America I see the Prospectus of the Cae Coch Mine bears upon it the name of our firm, together with those of three directors who are entirely unknown to us and who appear to have no connection whatever with the names submitted to me when you asked whether my firm would act as auditors.

It is our practice never to connect ourselves with companies unless we have some previous knowledge of the directors and we regret you should have put our names upon the Prospectus without having previously informed us of the changes you have made.

We must make our enquiries respecting the gentlemen who are connected with the concern and will write you later. In the meantime we

are not in a position to comply with your request as to giving a certificate on the accounts of the character required.

A little later we find in regard to this particular flotation:

We very much regret that it is not in our power to improve the
report we have already made. The facts are stated truthfully as we find
them: we can understand the desire of the directors to have a fuller and
unqualified certificate but no chartered accountant would, in our opinion,
be justified in giving one on the data supplied to us.

Prospectus reports at that period fell short of modern
standards. In a report given by the firm in 1890, profits were
stated thus:

The profits for the first half of this period, viz. the five years to 31st
December 1884 were, on an average £49,372. 0. 2. per annum.

The profits for the second half of this period, viz. the five years to
31st December 1889 were, on an average £60,372. 5. 9. per annum.

The profits for the first year in the series of ten years, viz. the year to
31st December 1880 were £31,399. 16. 2.

The profits of the last year in the series of ten years, viz. the year to
31st December 1889 were £64,732. 18. 2.

The profits of the ten years compared one with another do not display any very remarkable fluctuations. The figures above quoted indicate
a considerable increase in the average yearly profits.

John Griffiths's views on the promotion of companies and
issues of capital were frequently sought by those who regarded
him not merely as a good accountant but as a shrewd and wise
man of business:

So far as I have enquired and can form an opinion there is not the
slightest chance of being able to float this enterprise as a joint stock
company in London.

The reasons given for dissuading a well-known brewer from

floating his business as a company are the opposite of those normally regarded as unfavourable:

My own view of the present position is that it is already good enough and that, apart from outside and personal reasons, the business is too good, too well managed and too well under control (without undue strain on your own energies) to make it at all desirable to sell, even in part. . . . In the meantime, as in all such cases, it would be well not to moot the matter until you are quite prepared to take action, if suitable terms can be arranged, as whispers on such a business, until a decision is reached, are likely to be damaging now or hereafter.

John Griffiths was consulted on a different kind of business by Miss Melnotte of the Royal Comedy Theatre, Haymarket, to whom he wrote:

I very much fear that it does not lie in my power to obtain you a tenant for the theatre. I will, however, enquire in the only likely quarter of my connection and let you know should anything result.

Miss Melnotte was a famous theatrical manageress, a contemporary of Henry Labouchere and John Hollingshead; the last named built in 1868 the original Gaiety Theatre where Gilbert and Sullivan's first work was performed.

Early Audit Reports

The auditors' report on the balance sheets of those days was commendably brief, the usual form being 'Audited and approved' or 'Audited and found correct'. On occasions the firm's signature appeared without comment. Sometimes there is a variation: 'We have examined and approved the above balance sheet and accounts' and in a report dated 29 June 1874 to the chairman, directors, and shareholders of the Spring Valley Coffee Co. Ltd. the firm wrote:

We have again to express our complete satisfaction with the manner in which the London Accounts of your Company are kept. We believe the Accounts to which we have this day affixed our signature exhibit a sufficient and true account of the Company's affairs, and of the working of the crop 1872–1873.

This seems to be the forerunner of the 'true and fair view' report of modern days. The somewhat bloodless reports were, however, frequently accompanied by letters to directors containing comments, criticisms, advice, recommendations, and commendation. To the Directors of the *Observer*, John Griffiths writes:

I am sorry to note a considerable falling off in the sale of the newspaper as well as in the advertisements. The advertisements were so heavy in the half-year to 31st December 1886 that doubtless the income may be regarded as abnormal; but the falling off in sales appears to me to be very important having regard to the future position of the paper. On the other hand I find the expenses have nearly all considerably increased. I particularly draw your attention to the sub-editorial and office salaries. There is also a considerable addition to the cost of reporting. You will know perhaps whether it is worthwhile to make any expenditure in pushing the paper either by advertising or by any other means. I need hardly suggest to you the importance of keeping up the circulation.

The *Observer* was one of the earliest of many newspaper clients.

Some pungent criticism must, we feel, have accompanied the following letter:

As auditors for the first time to your company we have had to refer to several matters which otherwise perhaps would not be within our province but these, as we feel sure you will understand, are not in any way intended to be offensive.

After discussing the merits of amortising the capital expenditure on a mine by setting aside a fixed amount per ton on minerals raised, a letter concludes:

As you are doubtless aware, in many undertakings such perfectly sound steps are not taken, but even if not adopted it is well to have the question discussed and the position understood.

On the other hand, an excessive prudence in the disposition of profits called forth the following comment:

I cannot understand why profits on Public Houses managed for the firm should be placed in reduction of goodwill. I should think that the goodwill should be treated as an asset and those profits added to the other profits for division.

John Griffiths was often consulted as to dividend distributions and other allocations of profits. The directors of the Buenos Aires Great Southern Railway must have felt a glow of pride when they read:

There is not a figure in the whole of the statistical statements which is not satisfactory to me. The whole out-turn is very creditable to all concerned and the shareholders have every reason to be contented and grateful to the very capable men conducting their affairs.

Sometimes there is a discordant note in the correspondence when clients were unwilling to pay a proper fee:

We are very desirous of continuing to perform the duties which we have undertaken for so many years but we are indisposed to do so at little or no advantage to ourselves which would be the result if we accepted your proposition.

Daily rates of charge in London had risen to 4 guineas for principals but remained stationary at $1\frac{1}{2}$ guineas for clerks, increased to 5 guineas and 2 guineas whilst in the country— surely very moderate advances over a period of thirty years. The firm was, however, prospering. In 1874 the fees totalled £7,597; in 1887 they amounted to £25,814, whilst in 1900 they reached £41,193. Expenses and salaries were moderate and the partners were able to enjoy a comfortable competence in the days when the golden sovereign was worth twenty silver shillings.

Extracts from directors' reports of 1888–90

The reports and accounts of some of the firm's old clients provide an interesting study of conditions in the latter part of the nineteenth century, and of events which now seem very far away. The board of the Langham Hotel, one of the firm's earliest clients, reported in 1888:

For a long time past the Directors have had under consideration the question of introducing the Electric Light into the Hotel, and, being now satisfied that this mode of lighting has, in the eyes of the travelling public, become a positive necessity, they have arranged for its introduction forthwith, at the same time retaining the present gas appliances intact to meet any possible contingency.

It is sad to think that the Langham Hotel has been converted into a block of office premises.

From the report of the Savoy Hotel for 1890 comes the following:

It may be remembered that the Directors were of opinion last September that it was not desirable to publish the accounts of the Hotel and this view was adopted by the shareholders but in consequence of many requests made by shareholders in the country who are unable to come to London to attend meetings they have thought it well to circulate privately among the shareholders the Balance Sheet and Profit and Loss Account.

Then follows a most depressing picture:

The expectations of the Directors to pay a dividend upon the Ordinary Shares out of the profits of the past year have not been realised, owing chiefly to the appalling weather of the last months of the year, the commercial depression and the general lack of money.

Such a spell of bad weather,—fog, frost and snow, more or less continuous, in January, February and March—has not been known for very many years and is hardly likely to recur. This cause, and the continuing commercial depression, have equally affected all first-class hotels and restaurants. The Directors are glad to note, however, that the receipts have greatly improved of late, although the effects of the influenza have caused them to be lower than they otherwise would have been. A large portion of the most valuable custom of this hotel is drawn from aristocratic and wealthy persons from the Continent, many of whom, who had actually engaged suites of rooms, have, during the last few weeks, cancelled their orders, and are not coming, assigning the fear of the epidemic as the reason.

In 1890 occurred the Baring crisis, when a financial catastrophe was only avoided by the prompt action of the Bank of England and the joint stock banks. (Some years later the firm became auditors of Baring Brothers & Co. Ltd.) In the previous year when wages were booming, the directors of the Powell Duffryn Steam Coal Co. Ltd. had told their shareholders:

Having regard to the critical state of the labour market the directors earnestly request that the shareholders will in their own interest consider this report strictly confidential. The question of labour is a most anxious one. The men in every possible way are agitating for increased wages and also are endeavouring to reduce the output, and by so doing, increase the cost.

At that time we find the firm writing: 'Please forward to us four tons of the best household coal to be delivered in the morning before business hours.' The cost was 23s. a ton.

Taxation work

There is hardly a mention of taxation work, perhaps not surprising with a rate of income tax in 1874 of 2d. in the £. That year, however, heralded a severe industrial depression. *The Accountant* of 1 October 1949, in a review of seventy-five years of income tax, gives a picture of citizens harrowed by taxation which makes amusing reading to a generation which has since had to pay up to 19s. 6d. in the £ during life with a duty of anything up to 80 per cent. on their deceased estates:

On 3rd July, 1874, by a large majority, the House of Commons carried the following resolution:

'That, in the opinion of this House, the continued imposition of the Income Tax, except in time of war or some great national emergency, is unjust and impolitic, and it is advisable that such Tax should be still further reduced and ultimately altogether repealed at the earliest possible period.'

The proposer of the resolution had drawn a harrowing picture of 'persons in the position of gentlemen' making piteous appeals to the Chancellor to give them time or to excuse them on the grounds that they did not know where to lay their hands on the money they were called upon to pay. At this time the rate of income tax was the lowest rate ever, and Gladstone, in his election campaign, had even promised to abolish the tax.

It was in the same year that Stephen Dowell's famous work *The Income Tax Laws* was first published, and his introduction to it contains this prophetic utterance:

'. . . of all taxes ever imposed . . . the income-tax is the most important. This importance it derives not so much from the amount of the present yield . . . as from its history and potentiality. The records of the tax are inscribed with a long list of victories in war and we may with confidence rely on its productive power in case of danger or necessity.'

Banks as limited companies

The year 1878 saw one of the financial sensations of the nineteenth century, the failure of the City of Glasgow Bank. At that date most of the principal banks held the view that to register as limited companies might impair their credit. The shock of the Glasgow Bank failure, which reduced a large number of its shareholders to penury, created a strong feeling against unlimited liability, and to avoid the wholesale selling of bank shares the Companies Act 1879 was passed permitting banks to register as limited companies with specified uncalled capital, and subject to compulsory audit. A letter received from the Midland Bank on 2 January 1946 recorded the centenary of the opening of the firm's account in the name of W. W. Deloitte on 2 January 1846, with the London Joint Stock Bank, which amalgamated with the Midland Bank in 1918. The firm acted as joint auditors of the London Joint Stock Bank from the date when it assumed limited liability in 1882 until the merger.

Office discipline

Office discipline was strict and any departure from the rules was visited with grave displeasure. Edward Allbeury seems to have come in for more than one reprimand; for instance:

On sending for you this afternoon about 5.40 I found you had left the office of the Barcelona Company without returning here. Surely you have been long enough in the office to know the regulations. The consequence of your breach in the rules is that I am obliged to defer my instructions to you and am unable to reply to an enquiry from one of the directors.

On this occasion Mr. Allbeury seems to have been able to vindicate himself for across the press copy of the letter is written in large letters in blue pencil with obvious satisfaction, 'Came back to office. E.A.' Letters couched in similar severe terms were addressed to a clerk who went from one audit to another without the firm's instructions: 'If you are not inclined to work seriously with us we do not require your assistance', and, 'We can find no excuse for your neglect of the office rules in recently absenting yourself from your work without permission or explanation. The matter shall be overlooked on this occasion but should you again offend we shall be compelled to dismiss you without considera-tion.' And again: 'I am much disappointed that you should apparently be so little acquainted with our office regulations that the assent of an official of our client is adequate authority for you to be absent from your duties without our permission.' Punc-tuality in attendance to duties was of first importance: 'The immediate cause of his leaving us was a want of punctuality.'

Delay in rendering monthly Time Summaries was a constant source of complaint: it may console others to know that William Plender and P. D. Griffiths were not exempt from strictures on this ground. To Mr. Plender the firm wrote: 'We must ask you to furnish to the Time Ledger keepers your time summary for March without further delay', and a telegram to P. D. Griffiths read: 'Extremely surprised at inattention to application for time summary. Must have it by morning.' When he sent it in it was returned for him to enter the folios!

Something went wrong with the abrupt dismissal of a commissionaire on the ground of 'slackness in the mornings due to the fact of his undertaking night duties after leaving our office', for we find a letter written post haste to the commanding officer of the Corps of Commissionaires containing a glowing tribute to Sergeant Flynn:

We very much fear we may have done some injustice to Sergeant Flynn who is leaving our service tomorrow. We have made full enquiry and desire to put on record that Flynn has done very well for us in the past six months. He is a good penman and his qualifications generally as a clerk have possibly led to some members of our staff expecting from him more than a commissionaire should be asked to do—this may have led to an observation that he was remiss at times. We beg you to treat this letter as a certificate in favour of Sergeant Flynn, his qualifications and industry as well as his invariable good manners and willingness to oblige.

Office rules and regulations

Some of the changes which have taken place since those now rapidly receding days are shown by a look at the office rules and regulations. Office hours have not altered appreciably—a reduction of half an hour daily by closing at 5.30 instead of 6, with an interval of 1 hour instead of 45 minutes for lunch. Only a skeleton staff now attends on Saturday mornings, compared with the old rule that 'Work permitting the office will be closed at 2 o'clock.' Annual holidays have been improved for senior staff and those with long service. The habit of smoking at work, unheard of in earlier days, is now the subject of a request 'to refrain from smoking in the corridors, at public inquiry counters and in the cashier's and general offices during office hours'. But perhaps the most important change has been recognition, since World War II, of the status of those members of the staff occupying the most responsible positions who are designated 'Managers' or 'Supervising Seniors' with privileges corresponding to their status. A contributory pension scheme was inaugurated in 1934. The advent of women has changed the phrase 'gentlemen of the staff' to 'members of the staff'. Lord Plender, speaking in 1934 on his observations on half a century of business life in the City, said:

When I first entered the City of London some fifty years ago to take up my duties in a chartered accountant's office, life was quieter; the pace was less lively; clerks dressed more soberly in a morning coat and silk hat; the scale of pay was appreciably lower and office hours were elastic with a tendency to longer rather than shorter working days. Access to the city for the ordinary toiler was by bus or steam service on the railways—no tubes, no taxis, no cars. We started earlier and reached home later. Recreation was not easily obtainable. The playing grounds which banks, insurance companies and large business enterprises now provide for their staffs in the suburbs were then unknown. Female clerks were not employed and it was a rare occasion to see ladies in the City streets. Luncheon facilities were less wholesome for the clerk, but prices for what was procurable were very moderate. All this has changed and we see today a new world hardly comparable with the old conditions I have briefly referred to. And among the changes I may also mention the architectural developments in transforming the appearance of historic thoroughfares like Lombard Street, King William Street, Cornhill, London Wall, Moorgate and Poultry.

Before his death Lord Plender was to see destruction and desolation in the City compared with which the developments were almost trivial. Many of the old eating-houses in the City fortunately remain, but the famous one, Crosby Hall, once a palace of Richard III, was moved from St. Helen's Place early in this century and re-erected on Chelsea Embankment.

J. G. Griffiths's work for the Institute and profession

John Griffiths was vice-president of the Institute in 1892–4 and in the two years 1897–9 was the second Deloitte partner to be elected president. The staff presented him with an illuminated address of congratulation, signed by seventy-eight members, on his second term of office. He was on the council for forty-two years, and continued to be a member, contrary to later practice, for twenty years after his retirement from business. Chairmen of committees now normally stay in office for three years, but he was chairman of the General Purposes Committee for seventeen years and of the Students' Society's Grants Committee for twenty-two years. He found time also to act as examiner for the Intermediate and Final Examinations. He was president of the Students' Society of London for eight years.

Mr. Griffiths's presidency coincided with the activities of one of the government committees appointed at intervals to consider amendments to company law. A letter to Mr. Edwin Waterhouse, a member of the council, on the views of another member, Mr. Welton, showed a shrewd appreciation of the need to move with the times:

I am afraid I shall require some convincing to induce me to concur in all Mr. Welton's suggestions.

He evidently is opposed to the intervention of the State to protect investors where a little business knowledge and some trouble would enable them to protect themselves. Well, I sympathise with Mr. Welton and agree with him that there is too much tendency to protect people at the expense of the Government who will not trouble to protect themselves. I fear there is no chance of succeeding in allaying the tendency in this direction of all modern commercial legislation and I therefore prefer to suggest improvements of the present system rather than a radical alteration of the existing law. When you have read and digested Mr. Welton's notes would you kindly pass them on to another Member of the Committee.

John Griffiths also endeavoured to counter what he considered to be encroachments of the bureaucracy into the professional fields of accountancy, by urging the Institute to oppose a Local Government Bill providing for the audit of the accounts of county councils by district auditors, and by refuting suggestions that the cost of bankruptcy and liquidation was less when carried out by government officials. Accountants were suffering at that time from the transfer of much profitable insolvency business to officials under the Bankruptcy Act 1883, and the proposed transfer of similar activities under the Companies Act 1900.

Mr. Griffiths contributed the article on Accountants in the first edition of the *Encyclopaedia Britannica* over the initials 'J.G.G.'

Retirement of Henry Dever

Henry Dever, whose health had been failing, retired from the partnership in 1897 and died two years later. His professional and other qualities were summarized in an obituary notice in *The Accountant* of which the following is an extract:

It is with much regret that we record the death, at the age of 63, of Mr. Henry Dever, of the firm of Messrs. Deloitte, Dever, Griffiths & Co., Chartered Accountants, 4, Lothbury, E.C.

Mr. Dever has been from boyhood associated with the firm in which he subsequently became a partner, and of which he has been a member nearly forty years. For the last two or three years his health has been failing, but it is only within the past nine months that he has been obliged to retire from active business life. He died on Sunday evening, the 4th July, quietly and painlessly.

Mr. Dever's name has been a household word in commercial circles in the City for close upon half a century and the ramifications of his business connections were deep and widespread.

He was engaged on many of the most successful enterprises of the last half-century and at the date of his death he was associated professionally with some of the largest insurance, railway and other companies.

Some years ago he acted as professional liquidator of the Briton Medical and General Life Association, Lim., and was also liquidator of the Great Eastern Steamship Co. Lim., and, lately he acted as joint manager and receiver and as liquidator of C. de Murrieta & Co. Ltd.

He had all those qualities of tact, decision, and readiness that go to make a successful chairman and the way he used to manage the stormy meetings in connection with the Briton Medical and General Life Association when the room would be packed with irate policyholders, was admirable in the extreme.

The profession as a whole would doubtless have seen more of Mr. Dever had not that gentleman considered that his firm was well and ably represented on the Council in the persons of Mr. W. W. Deloitte and Mr. J. G. Griffiths (the present President of the Institute of Chartered Accountants). Still, his influence in the world of accountancy is abundantly manifest in the persons of many members of the profession who were fellow workers with him, amongst whom may be mentioned, Mr. J. J. Saffery, Mr. J. Gane, &c. &c. In fact the firm of Deloitte, Dever, Griffiths & Co., and the late firm of Quilter, Ball & Co. have long been noted as the nurseries from which have sprung the most eminent accountants in the country.

Mr. Dever was fond of country life and a few years ago built a place at Farnborough, in Hampshire, and it was at Farnborough Court that he passed away. He took considerable interest in local affairs and was the first Chairman of the District Council and sat regularly on the Aldershot Bench. He gave a recreation ground to the parishioners and in other directions conduced to their welfare.

Few men inspired more regard and affection than he, and no one more than his brethren in the profession will be readier to extend to Mrs. Dever their sincerest sympathy in her bereavement.

One more link is thus broken in that chain of accountants who, in their day, controlled large matters. With their rise was that of accountancy and few, even among the great names of the past, had wider experience, better judgment and rarer qualities than Mr. Dever.

C. de Murrieta & Co. Ltd.

The insolvency of C. de Murrieta & Co. Ltd. was a result of the Baring crisis. There is a report in *The Times* of 31 January 1894 of the public examination of the officials and directors of the South American and Mexican Co. Ltd., a company with which the affairs of Murrieta & Co. were involved. It was a *cause célèbre* of the day: many eminent counsel were engaged and the Bank of England was represented. Henry Dever successfully underwent a long examination and cross-examination. To assist in the liquidation Dever engaged an employee of Murrietas, F. B. Evans by name, who remained with the firm for forty-five years. A staid bachelor with Dundreary whiskers, he was a highly respectable and respected gentleman of a bygone age. The staff, with a shrewd sense of the ludicrous, christened him 'Biddy'. He went yearly to Paris where, it was said, he would suggest to his juniors that they should retire early so as to be fresh for the next day's work; but a wag spread the story that when they later emerged from their bedrooms to enjoy the night life of Paris, Mr. Evans was also seen sneaking down the hotel stairs.

73

Admission of William Plender to partnership

The retirement of both Deloitte and Dever in 1897 reduced the partners to two and William Plender was admitted to the firm after serving for thirteen years on the staff.

William Plender was trained in the office of John G. Benson & Co., Newcastle upon Tyne, and after passing the final examination of the Institute in 1883 sought his fortune in London with nothing more than a letter of introduction from Mr. G. B. Monkhouse, a practising accountant in Newcastle. He never tired of relating how he came to accept the offer of employment made to him by John Griffiths in preference to that of another large London firm which was willing to engage him at £2 a week, against £100 per annum offered by John Griffiths. He accepted the lower remuneration as being a more gentlemanly proposal—in the light of William Plender's subsequent career, an instructive example of the influence of trivial incidents on the future course of events.

Admission of P. D. Griffiths to partnership

In 1898 P. D. Griffiths returned from the New York Office to become a partner in the London firm.

The Period 1901–1956

End of the Victorian era

THE turn of the century brought the approaching end of the Victorian era. Great as the betterments in social conditions and material progress in Great Britain had been, the next half-century was to see still greater reforms coupled with mechanical inventions which were to revolutionize the way of life to a greater degree than had been imagined possible. The pattern of business, both domestic and international, underwent great changes which considerably widened the scope of practising accountants' duties and activities.

In 1900 a new Companies Act had been placed on the statute book which, like each succeeding Act, made compulsory the audit of the accounts of all companies, though it was not until 1947 that it was enacted that auditors of companies (other than exempt private companies) must be members of bodies of professionally qualified accountants named in the Act or approved by the Board of Trade. The Boer War and the Russo-Japanese War had little effect on business though the commercial supremacy of Great Britain was gradually being challenged. The firm possessed in increasing degree the confidence of governments at home and abroad, and a steadily growing clientele, many with household names, in every part of the world. Until 1897 there had never been more than four partners at any one time. The new century was to see the emergence of a much larger firm and its development as an entity to a much greater degree than hitherto.

Retirement of J. G. Griffiths

In 1902 John Griffiths retired at the comparatively early age of 57, and three more partners who had been members of the staff for some years were introduced, Edward Davis, Lionel Maltby, and Herbert Guedalla. (Incidentally, the firm had earlier omitted to register the articles of clerkship of Edward Davis with the Institute for nearly three years, but after due apology the omission was overlooked.) The services and experience of John Griffiths were greatly in demand after his retirement and he was for many years a director of the Great Western Railway and other companies. It was the practice of the Great Western Railway to name locomotives after its directors and one engine was called the 'John G. Griffiths'. Its photograph used to adorn the firm's office but has disappeared. It is to be hoped that the engine also has been replaced by one with a more suitable and romantic name! Apart from Mr. Griffiths's continued activity on behalf of the Institute, he became joint honorary treasurer of the Prince of Wales' Hospital Fund for London (later King Edward VII's Hospital Fund for London) founded in 1897, the year of Queen Victoria's Diamond Jubilee, for the support, benefit, and extension of the hospitals in London. The firm are auditors to the fund. He designed a uniform system of hospital accounts and was created a Member, and subsequently a Companion of the Royal Victorian Order for his services to the fund. Mr. Griffiths died in 1922; a tribute to him by Lord Plender, published in *The Accountant*, after reciting many activities already outlined in this volume, concluded:

He was the trusted confidant and sagacious adviser of many clients, who were attracted to him not only for his high qualities as an accountant, for his keen and detached intelligence, but also by his character and personality.

My first acquaintance with Mr. Griffiths began in 1884 when, after passing the Final Examination of the Institute, I was engaged by him as a member of his firm's staff. He was kind and considerate to the stranger who came to him with an introduction to seek employment and that memory will always be gracious. From then until 1902, when he retired from the firm, and until his death I rejoiced in his friendship. Never did I hear him speak unkindly to anyone or of anyone. He had the rare gift of friendship—not too freely or indiscriminately offered, but once given and deserved it remained unchanging, steadfast and loyal. Those friends who felt the spell of his influence had their aspirations quickened, their sympathies enlarged and selfishness expelled. His staff rendered him devoted service and he deserved and kept their respect and admiration.

Mr. Griffiths's home revealed a cultivated taste in things beautiful. He sought the best in English and French literature. Widely read, disciplined, and strengthened by quiet reflection and having travelled much he carried about with him an atmosphere of tolerance and sympathy, of faith and charity. The most courteous of hosts, he delighted in hospitality. His benefactions were many and wide; no call upon his generosity was too heavy and not a few men owe to him new opportunities in life which his assistance rendered possible. Life with many is a rough voyage on an uncharted sea; with him the course was clear from the harbour-mouth and he piloted his barque to the desired haven.

There has passed from the roll of members of the Institute one of its supremely outstanding figures, who assisted in no small way in moulding its destinies, in building up its fortune and in making accountancy a great profession.

Mr. Griffiths's portrait, painted by A. E. Elmslie, hangs in the Institute with those of other presidents who have rendered exceptional service to the profession.

5, London Wall Buildings

It soon became apparent that the firm had outgrown the offices at Lothbury, which had not only become old-fashioned but were in any event about to be rebuilt. The staff then numbered 125: a lady typist, the forerunner of many others, had been engaged in 1902; and the days of the two male copyists, pens behind ears, with their beautifully written but slowly produced copper-plate accounts (though one of them habitually breathed an aroma of whisky after lunch) were coming to an end. It is now difficult to imagine how business was conducted in those days when copies of all accounts and other documents were separately written out in long hand.

In 1905 a move was made to 5, London Wall Buildings, then the latest design in offices, newly erected by the wealthy South African firm of Wernher Beit & Co. Although a little way from the centre of the City, the new offices were pleasantly placed in Finsbury Circus, a situation still calm and quiet except when a brass band plays in the Circus gardens on Wednesday mornings! A member of the staff at that time who was present at the move can still remember the surprise and apprehension with which the clerks saw the brass plates at the door at No. 5 indicating the offices of Deloitte, Plender, Griffiths & Co.: it was widely believed that the change from the thirty-two-year-old style of the firm—Deloitte, Dever, Griffiths & Co.—would irretrievably damage its goodwill.

London Wall Buildings
(Entrance to No. 5)

The Bank of England, 1956

Finsbury Circus gardens have never been built on. In Roman and medieval times they were a dumping place for rubbish tipped over the City wall and the Guildhall Museum contains many examples of pottery and metal ware dug up when the Metropolitan Railway was constructed under the open space.

Recollections of 4, Lothbury in the nineties

Before we leave the memories of Lothbury it is fitting to record some impressions of a former member of the staff, Harold E. Gibb, for many years head of the Registration and Share Transfer Department, who retired on 30 June 1949 after fifty-two years' service. We take the following from notes prepared by him in 1941:

'Deloittes of the Nineties'—yes, that conjures up many memories but when one remembers that the firm was started in 1845, nearly a century ago, it does not seem that the 'nineties' are really so very far away and yet the age has so completely changed that looking back, as I do now, it sometimes seems a very long time indeed.

I do remember, however, as though it were yesterday, the day when I was brought to the office by my father to be interviewed and judged as to whether I was a fit and proper person to be initiated into the intricacies of indexing letter books and the keeping of stamps. I was only fifteen and it was my first visit to the City, the date was Wednesday, 15th December 1897, and I started off in the General Office on the following Monday morning, at 4, Lothbury. What a quaint old place it was; I must own to a slight sense of disappointment—you see I was a very young fifteen and I had imagined an enormous building with hundreds, possibly thousands of clerks, all hard at it for very life. But what did I find? Very few people indeed, for the staff then numbered only seventy and naturally most were out and about the clients' business.

And what of the City itself—the throngs of silk-hatted men, the packed crowd ever in Throgmorton Street when the Stock Exchange was busy with the South African gold boom, the steady rumble of the horse-drawn buses with their iron-rimmed wheels, the jingle of the bells on the horses of the hansom cabs, the gas-lit streets, and the general air of comfortable ease and prosperity over all. And in the evenings, in the West End, crowds of well-dressed men and women crowding the streets and theatres. Irving at the Lyceum, Maskelyne & Cooks at the Egyptian Hall, and at the Queens Hall was commencing the first season of the Promenade Concerts. [*The reference to Maskelyne & Cooks, the famous magicians, recalls the fact that a youngster who joined the staff later became the secretary and subsequently a vice-president of that exclusive body, The Magic Circle. We hasten to add that this achievement was in no way due to his training in Deloittes!*]

The entrance to the old office at Lothbury was a narrow doorway which looked down Princes Street, and a long dark wooden passage led to some stairs which, in turn, led to the office itself. The general office and the partners' rooms were on this 'first floor' and there were two floors above. The top floor consisted of but one room and it was called the 'May Office' because a company named The May Consolidated Gold Mining Co. Ltd. was lodged there.

Electric light had recently been installed and I remember a considerable rivalry as to who could obtain the luxury of a 16 candle power lamp over the ordinary variety which was but a meagre 8.

It would be hard today to imagine Deloittes without its complement of typists, but in those early days of mine, no such thing as a typewriter was seen, or would have been tolerated in the office. Mr. Edward Davis gave me my first job of fair copying. I recall thinking of him on that first occasion as quite an elderly gentleman. I have since realised he must have been 28 or 30! Teddy Davis, as he was always called, was the captain of The Lothbury Cricket Club, a product of Deloittes in the 'nineties'.

Many things spring to my memory of those far off times which go to make one realise the difference between the methods obtaining then and the progress since, bringing with it speed and efficiency undreamed of in the 'nineties'. There was, for instance, only one telephone which was in a little alcove adjoining the general office. The number, I remember, was Avenue 705. It was considered quite an adventure to speak over it. Whoever was asked for had to be summoned and fetched, for 'extensions' were unknown and of course there were no lifts. There were, however, 'speaking tubes' connecting some of the remote rooms with the general office. Great experience and much care was needed to handle these labour-saving devices, for the innocent and unskilful was apt to receive a mouthful of dust and air from one of his youthful colleagues playing a trick at the other end and who usually managed to remain anonymous.

I remember too the work of filing the papers was entrusted to one of the boys when he had some spare time! The letters and papers were all stuffed into drawers in one of the desks in the General Office and when there was opportunity, and the desk was full enough, it was the duty of the boy to fold and endorse them and stow them away in their proper boxes. I could go on setting out and recording many things that today would seem quaint and old-fashioned. I remember being terribly intrigued and interested in a square envelope which used to appear every evening, addressed to our then senior partner, Mr. J. G. Griffiths. In this envelope, which at first seemed to be absolutely empty, was a tiny card, not much bigger than a postage stamp, and I afterwards discovered that on the little card was written a note of Mr. Griffiths's engagements for the following day. This had to be posted to him, without fail, every evening.

Talking of posting letters. I remember a dreadful disaster when a new boy in an excess of zeal and anxiety to be quick about the mission entrusted to him, posted his entire load in an orderly bin which was near by!

In 1898, Mr. Percival Griffiths came to London from New York and took his place as the fourth partner. There was not much space to spare in that old office at Lothbury, and I remember a room which was at the top of the first flight of stairs being prepared for him. It was a dark little place, with the walls of another building only a little way from the one small window which, on a really fine day, had been known to admit a glint of daylight.

Of what worth are the impressions of little more than a schoolboy of these outstanding figures? Like most young people, I saw them all as quite old gentlemen. Of Mr. J. G. Griffiths, I recall his ever courteous manner and dignified bearing, his saying on one occasion—'We treat you all as gentlemen—we expect you to behave as gentlemen'; and in a lighter vein, coming up to us in the General Office—'If you're not busy, pretend you are'—a piece of advice I have often passed on to others. Mr. J. G. Griffiths would not have smoking in the office on any account and even outside it was frowned upon—well, perhaps a cigar or even a cigarette, but a pipe, never. In Mr. Cloutte, I remember a jolly round-faced man, more like a gentleman farmer than a professional man, walking about the office with his hands in his cross-cut trouser pockets, and telling the youngsters on a fine Saturday to get off as soon as they could, but hours were longer in those days—one went to lunch on Saturdays and the office closed at 2 o'clock, though very shortly it was changed to one. [*Mr. Cloutte retired in 1904.*]

Who shall say that the May Office did not give birth to the first office tea club in the City! It certainly did give birth to such a horror and I, unfortunate youth, was the Pooh-Bah in connection therewith. I was elected, willy nilly, to the posts of Managing Director, Secretary, Treasurer, caterer and washer-up. The subscription was 6d. a week, and with this high financial backing I was expected, nay, it was demanded of me, that I should provide tea, sugar, biscuits and condensed milk for five every afternoon. In the summer, fuel had to be provided in the shape of methylated spirit which necessitated the building up of considerable reserves. I used to resign every Friday, but it was no good, I was always re-elected with marked enthusiasm and firmness on the following Monday.

In a preface to Mr. Gibb's brochure, Lord Plender—known to generations of the staff as 'W. P.'—wrote:

They were, on the whole, happy years with successes and failures mingling and I remember so well how hard it was to climb the ladder that led to a Partnership. The rises seemed to come very slowly and for small sums, and when the Allotment craze was lively there was over-time which, being paid for at a higher scale than the normal salary rate, led to no lack of volunteers. I recall more than once this special class of work being continued without break for forty-eight hours, as the directors wished the Allotment Letters to go out quickly in case of withdrawal of applications for shares. There was rejoicing at the end of the month when the salary cheques were distributed.

The years have passed in quick succession; the business has expanded far beyond the expectations of early days and the prestige of the firm has advanced greatly. And the Partners of today acknowledge, with feelings of gratitude, the loyalty and help received from the staff in the steady and widening growth of the firm's business, its standing in the profession and in the financial and commercial life of the country.

Office functions

Before World War I it was the custom for the firm to give an annual smoking concert for the staff, to which the secretaries and accountants of many client companies were invited. It must be admitted that these functions were apt to become lively. The staff themselves, every now and then, ran a purely staff dinner to which some past members were invited. Dinner jackets were compulsory and the party was done in style, as evidenced by the menu reminiscent of those spacious days of one such function held at the Hotel Russell in 1911:

Huîtres Natives

. . .

Consommé Monte Carlo
Crème Longchamps

. . .

Turbot bouilli, Sauce Mousseline
Whitebait

. . .

Ris de Veau braisé Financière

. . .

Salle d'Agneau Jardinière
Pomme Rissolées

. . .

Poulet de Surrey en Casserole
Salade

. . .

Bombe Napolitaine
Corbeille de Friandises

. . .

Dessert

. . .

Café Noir

. . .

The programme of music included four artists and the chief
toast was 'The Firm'. The cost of this function was 10s. 6d. per
head, exclusive of drinks, and one cannot help thinking that as
the owners of the hotel were clients, and the chief staff organizer
was in charge of the audit, there may have been some price concession! According to signatures on a programme the dinner was
attended by sixty-two persons.

Between the wars the firm gave either a smoking concert or
a dinner each year. The former at which well-known variety
artists appeared, was favoured by the staff. In recent years an
annual dinner dance has been held at Grosvenor House at which
the members of the staff and their wives number about 700.
Occasions for sporting activities were necessarily restricted.

Edward Davis presented a golf cup and Arthur Cutforth gave a tennis cup, both competed for annually with replicas for the winners, but following the Second World War these events have unfortunately fallen into abeyance as have also the cricket matches with Cooper Brothers & Co. played with much friendly rivalry. Deloittes were able to put in the field a member of the staff who had played for a county and our opponents brought down a first-class cricketer, also believed to be a county player, from their Liverpool office: some thought this to be of doubtful validity and that he lacked the regional qualification to play! These and occasional matches between office sides were very good fun.

Imperial Tobacco Co. (of Great Britain & Ireland) Ltd.: British American Tobacco Co. Ltd.

The twentieth century has been notable for the rise of big business units as we know them today and among the first of these giants was the Imperial Tobacco Co. (of Great Britain & Ireland) Ltd. formed in 1901 to counter the price-cutting campaign in the British market inaugurated by the most powerful tobacco combine in the United States. Following cessation of this intensive competition the Imperial Tobacco Company's export business was sold to the British American Tobacco Co. Ltd. which was formed by the Imperial Tobacco Company and the American combine. In this manner it was arranged that each of the rival combines should retain its home market while the export trade of both was controlled by a single organization, an arrangement that has proved itself to be of considerable benefit to the shareholders and to this country. The firm has been closely associated with the Imperial Tobacco Company and the British American Tobacco Company since their inception.

Metropolitan Water Board: Port of London Authority

The early years of the century also saw the growth of public ownership of public utilities. In 1903 the Metropolitan Water Board was constituted by merging the water companies which supplied London. A few years later, in 1909, the Port of London Authority was constituted by Parliament to take over the dock companies. In both these cases Mr. Plender, as he then was, acted for the purchasing authority and the firm has since held the appointment as auditors of the Port of London Authority now made annually by the Ministry of Transport and Civil Aviation.

London Transport

In 1903, largely due to the foresight and enterprise of an American railroad magnate, C. T. Yerkes, construction began on a network of underground tube railways, and the old underground lines were electrified. The firm has been associated with the parent concern, the Underground Electric Railways Company of London Ltd., and with its successors in all the subsequent stages through which it and its undertakings have passed. Under the able direction of Albert Stanley (later Lord Ashfield), a Yorkshireman, who had been general manager of the New Jersey Transport Organization in the United States, the traffic of London, both underground and on the surface, was rescued from threatened chaos. The system was unified and co-ordinated in 1933, with other means of public transport, by the creation of the

London Passenger Transport Board. On nationalization, the railways and road services controlled by the Board were vested in 1948 in the British Transport Commission, but the administration and development of transport services in London were delegated to the London Transport Executive. L. C. Hawkins, a former member of the staff, is one of the members of the London Transport Executive and his services have been in demand by Commonwealth and Colonial governments to advise them on their transport problems.

Singapore Docks: United States Postal System

Other work in the first decade of the century included a visit by Mr. Maltby to Singapore on behalf of the Colonial Office in connexion with the purchase of the docks and foreshore for a naval station; and an examination, undertaken by New York Office on behalf of the Government of the United States, of the postal system of the Union. The instructions for this work were contained in a letter dated 17 April 1907 from the United States Senate Committee on Post Offices and Post Roads, signed by W. R. Andrews, as secretary, and approved by Boies Penrose, as chairman, in the following terms:

Gentlemen, By direction of the Joint Commission authorised by Congress to investigate the entire business system of the Post Office Department and the Postal Service, acknowledgment is made of the receipt of your communication of 12th instant proposing to undertake a complete investigation of the subject of Post Office systems of accounting and business administration and the terms upon which you are prepared to undertake the work, and to advise you that the Commission accepts your proposition.

Shortly before this inquiry, in 1905/6, New York Office enlisted the aid of staff from London Office to assist them, in collaboration with other American firms of accountants, in what was known as the Hughes insurance investigation. This investigation is stated in *The First Fifty Years—1895–1945*, a privately published review of the practice of Haskins & Sells, to have rocked the financial world and to have led to comprehensive revisions in the accounting methods of life insurance companies. This is believed to be the first occasion on which the firm collaborated with Haskins & Sells, with whom we subsequently formed a close friendship and alliance.

South African Office: Rand Water Board: South African war stores scandal

Towards the end of 1904 the firm received instructions to assist the British post-war government of the Transvaal in connexion with the formation of a Rand Water Board, probably inspired by the example of London, to take over the private water undertakings on the Witwatersrand. Mr. Maltby proceeded to Johannesburg to supervise the investigation. About the same time a South African partnership was formed in association with Annan Dexter & Co. of London under the style of Deloitte, Dever, Griffiths, Annan & Co. (now Deloitte, Plender, Griffiths, Annan & Co.). The first assignments of the South African firm were to complete the Rand Water Board inquiry and to investigate, in conjunction with Annan, Dexter & Co., on behalf of the Royal Commission on War Stores in South Africa, the accounts and transactions of what was then described as 'the War stores scandal'. With two such important engagements the South

African firm was launched on what has since proved to be a highly successful career: its large clientele includes a number of bodies under government auspices, e.g. the South African Reserve Bank, the South African Broadcasting Corporation, and the Industrial Development Corporation of South Africa. One of the first clients, an English company developing property in the suburbs of Johannesburg, paid a delicate compliment to Deloittes by naming two streets 'Lothbury Road' and 'Finsbury Avenue'. The firm occupies offices in Johannesburg in a large building named Annan House after John Annan the founder of the firm of Annan, Dexter & Co. London partners from Deloittes and Annan Dexters made extended visits to Johannesburg in the first years of the firm there and Arthur N. Smith, who had been articled to Deloittes in London in 1895, became the first resident partner and is still acting in that capacity. Arthur Smith is the sole remaining link with W. W. Deloitte and Henry Dever whom he recalls seeing whilst he was a junior in London Office. The business has now six branches in the Union of South Africa—Johannesburg, 1906; Cape Town, 1907; Durban, 1908; Port Elizabeth, 1929; Pietermaritzberg, 1936; and East London, 1938. There are eight branches in the Federation of Rhodesia and Nyasaland—Bulawayo, 1905; Salisbury, 1910; Ndola, 1931; Blantyre, 1948; Lusaka, 1950; Umtali, 1951; Kitwe, 1952, and Gwelo, 1955. Limbe Office opened in 1932 was closed in 1933. The total staff in the Union and Federation is 332. In Rhodesia the firm numbers amongst its clients the Reserve Bank of Rhodesia and Nyasaland, the Electricity Supply and Iron and Steel Commissions of Southern Rhodesia, and many agricultural and other boards of control, and audits the accounts of the large mining companies in the copper belt and of the British South Africa Company, known as the Chartered Company, which exercised sovereign powers over the Rhodesias until 1923. Since World War II the South African firm, in partnership with Gill & Johnson, practises under the style of Deloitte, Plender, Gill & Johnson at Nairobi and Mombasa in Kenya, at Kampala in Uganda, and at Dar-es-Salaam, Iringa, and Mbeya in Tanganyika. It is interesting to note that in the early years of the South African firm they consulted a young barrister named Smuts, to advise on the rejection of a London partner's claim for admission to the local society of accountants. He afterwards became Field-Marshal Smuts.

Mexico City Office

In 1906 a branch of New York Office was opened in Mexico City mainly to handle the important oil, railway, and other interests in Mexico of S. Pearson & Son Ltd., the well-known contractors and industrialists, old and valued clients in London. Lord Cowdray, the head of Pearsons, took into his organization many men who had been trained in Deloittes, prominent amongst whom was John H. Macdonald, a brilliant Scottish chartered accountant who ultimately became a leading figure in the many companies forming the Pearson group.

Work in Russia

In the opening years of the century the firm had a considerable clientele in Russia and it was usual for a group of clerks to proceed to that country to audit the accounts of clients carrying on business in places as far apart as St. Petersburg (now Leningrad), the Urals, and the Caucasus, and to investigate and report on oil, mining, and trading ventures in need of capital. The firm kept fur-lined coats and fur caps in storage to equip the staff on these visits. Stories were told of gargantuan Russian hospitality lasting well into the early hours and on one occasion one of the firm's representatives returned to London after a period in hospital, with a permanent reminder of his visit in the shape of a scar on his forehead, the result of a brawl with a cossack! A large amount of British capital was flowing into Russia and in 1911 Mr. Guedalla relinquished his partnership to become managing director of a company formed by London financial interests to take advantage of the immense potentialities of that country. In 1913 the firm decided to open an office in St. Petersburg where premises were taken in the famous Nevsky Prospect, with Stanley C. Wyatt as resident partner. Later a small office was opened in Moscow. Under Russian law it was not permissible for the name of a deceased partner to form part of a firm's name so the new partnership practised as Plender, Griffiths, Wyatt & Co. James Kilpatrick's first association with Deloittes was as an original member of the staff of the Russian office where he remained until the outbreak of World War I: he wrote a fascinating story of his experiences in Russia and of the firm's business there under the title of *Russian Interlude*. After the revolution of 1917 the Russian offices were forced to close down and the British staff were successfully brought home in somewhat hazardous circumstances. Stanley Wyatt later became Sir Stanley Wyatt and the British member of the Ottoman Public Debt Council.

'Soap Trust' litigation

Another matter which attracted considerable attention was the libel action brought in 1906 by Lever Brothers Ltd. against the Harmsworth Press regarded as a *cause célèbre* of the day. There was a great array of eminent counsel. The *Daily Mail* and its associates had been conducting an intensive campaign against the so-called Soap Trust, alleging victimization of the public by attempts to corner the market and by overcharging for reduced weight, and they advised their readers to boycott the Lever products. The firm was instructed by the newspapers concerned to investigate the amount of damage caused to Levers by the press campaign, and resulting falling off in sales. This was apart from a vast depreciation in Lever Brothers shares. Before disclosures were made in evidence, and probably to avoid publication of figures which might have proved detrimental to their business, Lever's accepted an offer of £91,000 damages—a sum then regarded as enormous.

Sir William Plender, *president of the Institute*

William Plender was knighted in 1911. He was the third partner of the firm to become president of the Institute of Chartered Accountants, which office he occupied in the two years 1910–12 at the early age of 49. *The Accountant* described his rise in the profession as being almost meteoric. He was the first president who had been admitted to the Institute by examination. It thus took thirty years for the old order of members, automatically admitted under the Charter in 1880, to give place to those who had passed the examination turnstile. To celebrate his election as president past and present members of the staff entertained Mr. Plender to dinner at the Carlton Hotel. In 1908 Mr. Plender had been chosen to represent the Institute at the Congress of American Accountants held at Atlantic City, N.J., the forerunner of subsequent International Congresses. During his presidency Sir William Plender was active in addressing members of the Institute and articled clerks in the various districts in which societies of members and students were established; his addresses to the Students' Society of London, of which he was president from 1909 to 1938, were models of clarity and wisdom, based as they were upon a real understanding of the problems of youth. Before the First World War he served on the Royal Commission on Railways and the committee appointed to inquire into the problem of Irish finance, and he was a Welsh church commissioner for twenty-eight years.

H. I. Chevalier: A. E. Cutforth: Buenos Aires and other South American Offices

In the period preceding World War I two further members of the staff were admitted as partners, Harry Ivyleafe Chevalier in 1907 and Arthur Edwin Cutforth in 1912. Chevalier, known as 'Chivvy', came to a sad end due to extravagance, and resigned in 1917. Cutforth had spent a year in Chile and Bolivia in 1908 on the affairs of a railway and at about the same time J. A. Pilling, another member of the London staff, had accompanied Baron Emile d'Erlanger to the Argentine in connexion with the many industrial undertakings whose capital issues on the London market had been sponsored by his firm. In view of the large and

93

growing number of companies with interests in South America
served by the firm in London, Mr. Pilling was asked during his
visit to explore the ground for opening an office in Buenos Aires.
Later in the same year an office in Buenos Aires was established
with Mr. J. Monteith Drysdale (whose own practice there was
absorbed) and Mr. Pilling as resident partners. The practice with
its large nucleus of London clients prospered and other offices
were opened: in the Argentine—Tucumàn (1912); Rosario
(1917); in Uruguay—Montevideo (1921); in Brazil—Rio de
Janeiro (1911); Recife (1917); San Paulo (1920); Santos (1921);
Porte Alegre (1953); in Chile and Peru—Santiago (1923);
Valparaiso (1923); Lima (1926); Arequipa (1952). Buenos Aires
Office has assisted several Argentine provinces and municipalities
by introducing new accounting systems and investigating their
financial positions. Mr. Pilling returned to London in 1923
where as a non-resident partner in the Argentine firm he was
responsible for liaison between the London and South American
firms until his death in 1942. In 1925 the practice of Sydney
Merritt & Co., established on the west coast of South America
for more than thirty years, was absorbed. Unfortunately the
subsequent political and financial vicissitudes of most South
American republics, together with economic difficulties on this
side of the Atlantic, have severely hampered the introduction of
British capital to develop their large latent resources, and have
also proved a deterrent to the recruitment of the firm's staff
now numbering 226. The nationalization of the Argentine
and Brazilian railways ended a long and intimate association
between them and the London and South American offices of
the firm.

The years 1910–11 produced three banking failures which, although relatively unimportant in their impact on the City, caused a stir at the time. The circumstances leading up to the liquidation of one of them, the Charing Cross Bank, are of interest as an example of one of those rare cases where the public interest overrides a professional man's duty of observing secrecy about his client's affairs. The sole proprietor of the Charing Cross Bank, named Carpenter, offered by extensive advertising a high rate of interest for deposits of £10 and upwards secured by surplus assets stated to be £371,000. In fact, there was an estimated deficiency of assets of £1,700,000 and interest was only capable of being paid out of incoming cash deposits. Accountants called in by Carpenter to investigate the large but unrealizable Canadian railway undertaking on which he had embarked advised him, in view of his state of insolvency, to inform the depositors and close the doors of the bank; but he refused to do so, hoping against hope that in the end his speculative ventures would turn out successfully. The accountants, after taking counsel's opinion, then consulted the president of the Institute, at that time Sir William Plender, who communicated with the Director of Public Prosecutions. The affair caused much distress among the 19,000 depositors who were mainly people of small means. Carpenter was sentenced to two years' imprisonment after the jury had made a recommendation to mercy 'on the ground of the age and optimistic temperament of the defendant'. The creditors appointed Sir William Plender as one of the joint trustees to wind up the so-called bank. Some years later he described the result of a visit paid by the trustees to Canada in connexion with the railway:

My second visit to Canada was many years after. I was a co-trustee in a large bankruptcy and one of the assets was an unfinished railway in the Gaspe peninsula south of the St. Lawrence river, about 100 miles in length. We required considerable capital to complete it which the estate could not find, but we arranged the finance with the Cabinet at Ottawa. The railway when completed was not a financial success and to our relief after many negotiations we sold the line to the Canadian National Railway with considerable benefit for the creditors in the estate.

One of the immediate reactions to the failure of the Charing Cross Bank was a run on the Birkbeck Bank which, like a previous run in 1892, was successfully met. The Birkbeck Bank was a substantial institution more akin to a building society than a bank, but it encountered financial difficulties some time later when it was forced to close its doors. The Court appointed Sir William Plender as Special Manager to assist the Official Receiver to wind up the bank's affairs; and the large premises in Holborn and the banking connexion were taken over by one of the joint stock banks. The third banking failure was the suspension of the Bank of Egypt which, although it caused considerable surprise, produced little effect in financial circles. Here again the Court appointed Sir William Plender to act as Special Manager and Mr. Davis spent some time in Egypt, where indiscreet advances to customers of the bank during the land boom had largely contributed to the failure. For many years afterwards a room at 5, London Wall Buildings in which the work of this liquidation had been done was commonly known as the Bank of Egypt.

Rubber boom 1910

The year 1910 saw the great rubber boom. For weeks on end there was a frantic rush to subscribe for rubber shares, many of which turned out to be valueless, but which were then being offered on prospectuses almost daily. Stockbrokers' offices closed their doors to the public whilst they endeavoured to deal with accumulations of orders. The firm's staff was kept busy for days and nights dealing with allotments and some of those who tried to work the clock round staved off sleep during the night by racing round Finsbury Circus. At the request of clients with extensive interests in rubber and produce from the East, the firm opened offices, in conjunction with George A. Touche & Co., under the style of Deloitte, Plender, Touche & Co., at Batavia (now Djakarta) and Surabaya in Java; these offices succumbed during World War I and were not reopened.

Doctors' remuneration in 1912

Controversies in 1956 about remuneration of doctors under the National Health Service remind us of an examination made by the firm in 1912, at the invitation of the Government, into the earnings of 'panel doctors' under the scheme then recently initiated by the National Insurance Act. The matter was of some political urgency and a large proportion of the staff was mobilized to inspect sample accounts of doctors in both urban and rural areas, who had agreed to have their books examined by an independent auditor. This must surely have been the beginning of what is now the National Health Service. One of the doctors remarked that dust after a dry spell enhanced his practice more than any other cause!

The story of Deloittes would be less than candid if it did not record a misfortune which befell the firm in 1913. It was referred to in *The Accountant*:

The annual meeting of the Law Guarantee Trust and Accident Society, Lim. (in Liquidation) was held on the 29th ult., when Sir William Peat, F.C.A., presided. Touching on the position of the auditors of the company, Sir William said that on the opinion of counsel as to their liability coming to their knowledge, the auditors immediately communicated with the liquidators as to terms of settlement, and met the situation in a highly honourable way, which relieved the society and liquidators of what would have been an expensive and lengthy litigation. There was a complete denial of liability on the part of the auditors, but in a spirit of compromise a settlement was proposed which was cordially approved by an eminent counsel consulted by the liquidators, and sanctioned by the Court. As a result, they had received the sum of £20,000 in settlement of a claim which might have amounted to £52,000.

It was alleged that the auditors had failed to report over-valuation of assets and understatement of losses on guaranteed mortgages taken over by the company. The firm was one of the first, if not the first, to cover itself by insurance against claims and had done so shortly before this happening: in view, however, of this early claim under the indemnity policy the partners voluntarily bore a substantial part of the amount and thus limited the recourse against the underwriters. Many years later, when the annual indemnity policy was being revised to meet new circumstances, it was submitted to Lord (then Sir John) Simon by the underwriters for his opinion. He is reported to have said he knew Lloyds underwriters insured many strange contingencies, but he did not know they gave blank cheques to the assured; a reference to a special clause in the original Deloitte policy which stipulated that any claim should be paid if the senior partner of the firm for the time being was of opinion that it would prejudice the firm to contest it.

Work in Ireland

The year 1913 saw the appointment of the firm as auditors of the Bank of Ireland and the years following brought a considerable amount of work in Northern Ireland where the Great Northern Railway of Ireland was already a client.

World War I

At the outbreak of war in 1914 the staff numbered 189, and many temporary clerks of both sexes were engaged during the following four years. Of 129 men of the permanent and temporary staff who served in the forces, 28 lost their lives. Their names, together with those of 24 killed in World War II, are commemorated in a War Memorial in the office. The volume of special work imposed a severe strain on the remaining partners and staff, though other physical inconveniences were negligible compared with those of the Second World War. Air raids on London were few and did not approach in intensity those experienced later: the roof of London Wall Buildings immediately above the offices received a direct hit, but no great damage was done. It was during the 1914–18 war that the profession was first called upon to deal with many matters and problems which till then had been outside the normal scope of a practising accountant's activities. Many accountants placed their services wholly or in part at the disposal of the Government and their financial and administrative experience in carrying out executive and other duties in various government departments was invaluable. Legislation imposed supervision and controls on almost every kind of business, particularly in connexion with war production. Accountants had to complete and certify countless forms and returns. Complicated taxation designed to restrict the 'profiteer' added to the already heavy burden on the accountant in practice. The staff was implemented by transient women clerks and men under and over military age; and it is to be feared that the quality of the firm's work, like that of other practitioners, suffered.

Control of enemy banks

One of the first acts of the Government was to place under control the large branches of the German banks (Deutche, Dresdner & Disconto-Geschellschaft) and Austrian banks (Anglo-Austrian & Laenderbank) which had carried on large international businesses in London. Sir William Plender was appointed Controller and he appointed partners of Deloittes and other firms as supervisors to assist him in co-ordinating the liquidation of the banks' affairs. Mr. Davis acted in this capacity at the Laenderbank and Mr. Maltby at the Dresdner Bank. The extent of the ramifications of these banks can be judged from the fact that their liabilities to British, Allied, and neutral creditors exceeded £28 m., their non-enemy assets aggregated over £23 m., and in addition they held securities for customers of a face value of £38 m. The liquidation was of necessity a slow and intricate business, hampered by internment of many of the banks' key staff of enemy nationality and by loss of others to the armed forces. Towards the end of 1916, after the publication as a government blue paper of a long and detailed report on the progress of the liquidation, Lord Northcliffe published a letter in *The Times* (then controlled by him) attacking the Chancellor of the Exchequer and Sir William Plender for what he considered to be delay in completing the winding-up. He wrote:

I have evidence that these businesses and all other enemy concerns could have been closed down without difficulty twelve months ago. If the Government would transfer to me the task of winding up the German businesses I will undertake to have half of them closed by January 1st and the remainder by March 25th.

His letter contained the following threat:

We have therefore decided to ask Sir William to withdraw from his connection with *The Times* and other newspapers if the Government policy of keeping alive the German business is to be continued.

To Sir William Plender he wrote:

The conclusion I have formed in regard to your attitude of maintaining German interests in this country is that you have many other matters on your mind and are not well acquainted with German aims and methods.

These allegations were categorically denied by Sir William who added:

I have no policy except that of performing to the best of my ability the duties which have been entrusted to me by His Majesty's Government. I cannot permit any considerations of personal benefit to myself or my firm to induce me to retire from a position to which I have been appointed by the Government, believing as I do that the result of such a step on my part would be to create an embarrassing situation and materially delay the conclusion of the process of winding up the London branches of these banks.

In due course the firm was removed from the position of auditors of *The Times* and of Associated Newspapers Ltd., which controlled the *Daily Mail* and other newspapers.

The following interesting commentary appeared in *The Economist*:

In *The Economist* of 18th November we called attention to the extraordinary action of Lord Northcliffe in visiting his displeasure with the policy of the Government with regard to the German banks on Sir William Plender, who was acting as their Controller under Government instructions, by depriving his firm of their office as auditors to *The Times* and other papers under Lord Northcliffe's control. We then ventured to observe that 'to penalise a professional man in his professional capacity because he is doing work, under Government orders, in a way that does not meet with one's approval is a most ill-considered way of trying to hit the Government through the private interests of a worker on its behalf.' Since then Messrs. Walter Leaf and R. V. Vassar Smith, two distinguished bankers [*respectively the chairmen of the Westminster Bank and Lloyds Bank*] who were requested by the Treasury to enquire into the manner in which the operations connected with the enemy banks had been handled, had issued a report in which they stated that the operations had been 'conducted with an ability and expedition reflecting the highest credit on Sir William Plender and the supervisors who had acted under him.' This being so, an apology from Lord Northcliffe might perhaps have been expected, or, at least, a withdrawal of his ill-considered intention. But not so. The report just published of the Associated Newspapers Ltd. states that 'Messrs. Deloitte, Plender, Griffiths & Co., the auditors, offer themselves for re-election. A shareholder has given notice to propose at the annual meeting the election of

. . . as auditors.' This announcement is doubly interesting, as showing (1) that Lord Northcliffe's persecution of a distinguished public servant continues after his conduct, in the manner criticised, had received a handsome testimonial from two gentlemen whose impartiality and competence to judge cannot be questioned, and (2) that the firm which has consented, under the circumstances, to succeed Sir Wm. Plender's as Lord Northcliffe's auditors is none other than the firm in which . . . the present Financial Secretary to the Treasury, is a partner. After Sir Wm. Plender's experience, it would seem that the new firm of auditors to the Northcliffe publications will only retain their position as such as long as the business of the Treasury is conducted in a manner approved of by Lord Northcliffe. Since Messrs. Deloitte, Plender, Griffiths & Co. are to be removed because Sir Wm. Plender, as Controller of the enemy banks, did not satisfy his Lordship, Messrs. ——'s tenure will evidently be shortlived if in the matter of taxation or anything else . . . [*the Financial Secretary to the Treasury*] is associated with any measure that is displeasing to Carmelite House. . . . Lord Northcliffe's action is no doubt based on a sincere desire to do what he believed to be best in the interests of the nation: but surely there ought to be somebody who can correct his evident ignorance of the proprieties of business affairs.

After Lord Northcliffe's death *The Times* was acquired by its present proprietors and the firm became once more the auditors of that famous newspaper.

Sir William Plender's public services 1914–18

Apart from professional engagements for government departments Sir William's voluntary services in the national interest, in recognition of which he was made a Knight Grand Cross of the Order of the British Empire in 1918, were greatly in demand by the Government during the war. The list of his public activities ranged over a remarkable variety of subjects; they included membership of government committees dealing with the organization of the telegraph service; liquor trade finance; Metropolitan Munitions; Clerical and Commercial Employments; Military Service (Civil Liabilities); Enemy Debts; Surplus Government Property Disposals; Company Law Amendment; Demobilization; and Clearing Office for Enemy Debts. He was appointed honorary financial adviser to the Board of Trade in 1918 and was chairman and later president of the City of London War Savings Committee from 1916 to 1941. Sir William's many activities early in the war gave rise to questions in the House of Commons which were reported in *The Accountant* on 28 November 1914:

In reply to a question asked in the House of Commons on the 18th inst. by Mr. Joynson-Hicks, who inquired what appointments Sir William Plender, F.C.A., had received from the Treasury since August 1st last, the Chancellor of the Exchequer stated that the Treasury had appointed Sir William controller of the German, Austrian and Turkish banks . . .; that he had been good enough to consent to serve on the committee on relief to British traders, in respect of debts abroad, and to place his very valuable advice at the disposal of the Government in connexion with some other questions. He added that Sir William would not receive any remuneration from the public funds in respect of any of these services. Replying to a similar question, the President of the Board of Trade stated that the only appointment Sir William Plender had received from his department was that of controller of Meister, Lucius & Bruning Ltd. to which he was appointed by the Court on an application made by the Board of Trade under the trading with the Enemy Act, 1914. Probably no one (except perhaps Mr. Joynson-Hicks) will regret that the Government has seen fit to avail itself so far as it has of the great experience of Sir William Plender during the present crisis.

The Imperial Ottoman Bank

The Imperial Ottoman Bank had also been placed under Sir William's control as a bank incorporated in Turkey, but its ownership was largely in British and French hands.

Navy, Army, and Air Force Institute

The war brought into existence an immense trading organization which eventually became known as N.A.A.F.I. (Navy, Army, and Air Force Institutes). This provided in place of private contractors, canteen and other facilities for the forces and their families, where married quarters existed, and organized entertainment for the fighting services. The profits in excess of requirements to finance the undertaking were used to provide comforts and amenities for servicemen. Deloittes were appointed auditors and during and after both World Wars the staff travelled widely to innumerable places where N.A.A.F.I. operated, including France, Germany, Italy, Cyprus, Ceylon, Singapore, and North Africa. Alan Rae Smith (who had left the firm's staff in 1913 to enter the office of a firm of well-known merchant bankers) was seconded to the position of chief accountant of N.A.A.F.I. in 1916 from the Royal Army Service Corps, which he had joined shortly after the outbreak of war; he had to organize all the accountancy work involved in the growth of the organization from zero to a vast trading corporation, which operates in peace-time on a reduced but still extensive scale relative to the size and locations of the forces.

Royal Commission on Sugar

In 1914 the country imported all its sugar supplies and the whole of the sugar beet crop came from Germany. This led to the appointment of the Royal Commission on Sugar which took complete control of the sugar industry in the United Kingdom. It purchased all raw sugar, resold it to the refiners, and supervised the sale of the refined sugar and other products. The firm acted for the Commission in this formidable operation and at a later date was appointed auditors to the British Sugar Corporation, an undertaking formed to amalgamate, under government auspices, the companies engaged in the manufacture and refining of sugar from home-grown sugar beet, an industry started after the 1914–18 war.

Commission for relief in Belgium: United Nations Relief and Rehabilitation Administration

New York Office was concerned, during both World Wars, with organizations for the relief and rehabilitation of sufferers from enemy occupation. Herbert Hoover, who later became President of the United States, was chairman from 1915 to 1919 of the Commission for Relief in Belgium, which he organized and administered at the request of the American and Belgian authorities. In this he had the assistance in Brussels of staff from New York Office up to the time when the United States came into the war. Mr. Hoover, who at that time had an office in London Wall Buildings, used to call upon Sir William Plender smoking a large cigar. In World War II the United Nations appointed New York Office to audit the accounts of the United Nations Relief and Rehabilitation Administration from its establishment in 1943 until it was wound up in 1949. The activities of U.N.R.R.A., conducted from a special office in Washington, were of great magnitude, involving an expenditure of nearly $4,000 m. It covered the large areas of hostilities in the Far East, where the audit was conducted from the United States, and in Europe, North Africa, and the Middle East, where it was undertaken by London Office. A temporary office was opened in Shanghai (with the firm's name in Chinese characters at the entrance) and staff from London Office were stationed for lengthy periods in Athens, Cairo, Paris, and Rome. The discomforts of immediate postwar travel severely tested the fortitude of the staff; Vernon A. Tudball, later a London partner, flying in 1946 from Warsaw (where sniping in the streets was still going on) to Prague, found himself unexpectedly on a Russian airfield at Dresden. He spoke no Russian and the Russians spoke no English. His night's entertainment in the Russian mess was on Kremlin scale, but he took off safely next morning for Prague.

Robert Kerr

The partners suffered a great personal loss through the death of Robert Kerr in October 1918, at the early age of 35, in the ill-fated S.S. *Leinster* which was torpedoed in the Irish Sea whilst he was returning from professional duties in Ireland. Robert Kerr qualified as a member of the Institute of Accountants and Actuaries in Glasgow in 1905 and had only been a partner for six months. At that time it was the policy of the firm that all partners should be members of the English Institute. The only way Robert Kerr could qualify as such was to become articled for five years and to pass not only the intermediate and final examinations in accountancy subjects, but also the preliminary examination to satisfy the examiners as to his standard of general education! This rigorous test for partnership in the firm is fortunately no longer enforced on members of the Scottish Institute. Robert Kerr's partners and wide circle of friends at the time would have endorsed the tribute paid to him in *The Accountant*:

He was an exceptionally able accountant—quick in discerning the material point of any problem, helpful in consultation, sound in judgment and was possessed of attractive personal qualities which attached many friends to him.

Absorption of Welton & Bond

Towards the end of 1918 the old-established practice of Welton & Bond (the successors of Quilter & Ball of the early nineteenth century) was absorbed, largely on the initiative and negotiating ability of Arthur Cutforth. The elderly partners in that firm had failed to secure a succession of younger men to succeed them, with the result that on the death of Mr. Welton (president of the Institute in 1891–2) there was only one partner, Richard C. Martin recently admitted from their staff, to carry on the business. Richard C. Martin was made a partner in Deloittes and the firm secured valuable additions to its clientele, including the head office in London of the Hudson's Bay Company, which had been incorporated by Royal Charter in 1670 under the title of The Governor and Company of adventurers of England trading into Hudson's Bay—a reminder of the days when the adventurous spirit of Englishmen was at its height. Nothing could be more fitting than the recent revival by the company of the ancient office of Grand Seigneur, and the induction of Sir Winston Churchill as the illustrious successor to previous holders of that office.

Chartered Companies

Since the inception of company legislation, the granting of new Royal Charters to commercial undertakings has ceased. The firm numbers amongst its clients five corporations, besides the Hudson's Bay Company, which still operate under Royal Charter: the Russia Company (1553), since the Russian revolution a shadow of its former greatness; the London Assurance (1720); the Bank of Ireland (1783); Peninsular & Oriental Steam Navigation Co. (1840); and the Chartered Bank (1853), until recently known as the Chartered Bank of India, Australia & China.

Conditions after 1914–18 war: Imperial War Graves Commission

The decade following the 1914–18 war brought its problems, its frustrations, and its opportunities. A changed and disturbed world was emerging after the stupendous sacrifices of life and material. The firm was appointed auditors of that unique organization, The Imperial War Graves Commission, whose duty it is to care for the resting-places in all parts of the world of countless numbers of the dead of the British Commonwealth of Nations of two great wars. In 1938 the Commission appointed Sir Alan Rae Smith, as he had then become, as a member of a special committee to review its expenditure.

Staff difficulties following war

It is not surprising that in the aftermath of the war the firm was concerned with a large number of liquidations, reconstructions, and amalgamations; the installation of modern accounting techniques, and advising on many complicated problems arising out of oppressive taxation. Members of the staff were in many cases among the last to be released from the forces owing to the value of their accounting and business experience at all stages of demobilization. Many of those ultimately released took up attractive positions in industry. It was difficult to recruit qualified clerks, as the flow of new entrants to the profession had almost ceased for over four years. The services of women were increasingly in demand. In order to improve the usefulness of clerks with little or no training, the firm arranged for them to study for and take an examination set by an independent tutor. At a later date this scheme was abandoned in favour of the policy of encouraging unqualified members of the staff to qualify as incorporated accountants. This did not require articled service entrance which was limited by the regulations of the Institute of Chartered Accountants.

Death of Edward Davis: Changes in partnership 1919–36

Edward Davis, a most popular partner and likeable personality, died in September 1919 at the age of 51, after a long and distressing illness which he bore with the utmost fortitude. Several new partners were admitted between the two World Wars: Russell Kettle, for ten years Lord Plender's secretary, on 1 January 1919; a month later, Alan Rae Smith (who returned to the service of the firm after his departure noted earlier); Harold Read in 1921; James Kilpatrick and Harold Hockley in 1925; John W. Baird in 1931; and Charles R. Goulder in 1935. Richard C. Martin retired in 1934 and Lionel Maltby retired, after thirty-four years' partnership, in 1936.

Bank of England

In 1919 the firm's connexion with the Bank of England was initiated by the preparation of a scheme of cost accounting applicable to the particular conditions of the Bank. Later this association developed into a close and continuous contact, although under the constitution of the Bank the question of formal appointment as auditors did not arise. During the changing pattern of financial and other business activities in succeeding years, the firm has not only been closely associated with the Bank's own internal audit but has been consulted by the governor on many occasions on matters outside the domestic economy of the Bank.

Dawes Committee: Reichsbank

When the Dawes Committee was constituted in the early 1920's to inquire into the question of German ability to pay the large reparations demanded of her after the first war, the Rt. Hon. Reginald McKenna, a former Chancellor of the Exchequer and the chairman of the Midland Bank, was given the task of estimating how much foreign currency Germany had obtained by selling German marks, in which large speculation had taken place but which eventually became valueless. After investigation lasting about a month, in which the firm took part with French, Belgian, and Italian accountants and a United States observer, a figure of £350 m. was established—only £20 m. in excess of an estimate made by Mr. McKenna before he left for Berlin. The chief speculators had been nationals of the United States, Holland, and Spain. A few months later the firm was instructed to examine the financial position of the Reichsbank in Berlin.

Prominent failures after World War I: City Equitable Fire Insurance Co. Ltd.: Sir Charles McGrigor & Co.: Donald Campbell & Co. Ltd.: Beecham Trust Ltd.

Overtrading, unjustified optimism, and speculation, sometimes accompanied by fraud and forgery in an attempt to retrieve the situation, caused several notorious insolvencies in the interval between the two World Wars. A partner in the firm was concerned as Receiver, Liquidator, or Special Manager in several of these cases. One of them was the failure of the City Equitable Fire Insurance Co. Ltd. where the immediate cause of the difficulties was a series of highly speculative financial dealings entered into under the direction of the chairman, including the purchase of unrealizable investments which were wholly unsuitable to the business of an insurance company. It transpired that large sums entrusted for investment to the company's stockbrokers, of which firm the chairman of the company was the senior partner, had been used for their own business and not invested, although the stockbrokers certified that they held the investments included in the company's balance sheet. The chairman was sentenced to a term of imprisonment and his firm was made bankrupt. The auditors were held to have committed a breach of duty in accepting the certificate of the stockbrokers, instead of either insisting on the securities being put in proper custody, or else reporting the matter to the shareholders. But although negligence was proved it was held that the auditors were protected by an article of the company indemnifying its officers against liability for negligence or breach of duty. Such a protection was annulled in the subsequent Companies Act. Another insolvency in which the firm acted was that of Sir Charles McGrigor & Co., army agents and bankers, which with a capital of only £6,000 had liabilities of £800,000, covered by assets of less than £300,000. After negotiations the War Office, which had not at any time inquired into the financial position of its accredited agents, provided funds to pay an additional dividend of 10s. in the £ to those depositors who were army officers. The liquidation of Donald Campbell & Co. Ltd. was remarkable for heavy claims and cross-claims resulting in extensive and expensive litigation between the liquidator and certain of the directors, in which numerous leaders and junior members of the Bar were briefed, so much so that it was jocularly suggested in Court that the Bar should erect a statue to Donald Campbell in the Temple precincts. The litigation produced a notable decision of the House of Lords concerning the competence of the House to hear an appeal on a question of costs. After a hearing by five Law Lords, the legal point at issue was considered to be of such importance that it was decided to hear the appeal again before an enlarged Court of seven Law Lords. The failure of the Beecham Trust, in which the firm also acted, followed the suicide of a colourful character, Jimmy White, and provided sensational news. Jimmy White, a Lancashire man who never attempted to disguise his humble origin or dialect, amassed a fortune by astute financial deals and became a well-known and popular public figure in horse-racing, the ring, and the theatre, where he spent money on a lavish scale. But a severe slump in the shares of an oil undertaking, in which he had speculated heavily, brought his company down. He shot himself in his office. Investigation disclosed that for some time previously he had countered his financial embarrassments by admitting his friends to syndicates which each of them thought, quite wrongly, consisted of ten participants only; by this means White collected substantial sums. The ultimate unravelling of these situations raised almost insoluble questions of priority and except in one instance they were compromised without recourse to the Court.

Gas and Electric Light Companies inquiries: Tokyo Electric Light Company

Amongst more constructive work undertaken by the firm during this period may be mentioned the inquiries made and evidence given before parliamentary committees on the revision of the sliding scale for gas charges and the introduction of basic prices and dividends for gas companies, also the inauguration of a sliding scale and basic price system for electricity undertakings in London. In 1928 Mr. Maltby, accompanied by James Anderson, who later became a partner in the New York firm, paid a visit to Japan to examine the accounts of the Tokyo Electric Light Company—said to be at that time the largest electricity undertaking in the world—for purposes of a prospectus. A devastating earthquake followed within a short time of the large and successful issue of capital.

King George's Jubilee Trust

In 1935 the firm, which had acted as auditors of King George's Fund for Sailors since its inception in 1917, became auditors of King George's Jubilee Trust, founded to commemorate the Silver Jubilee of King George V, to care for the welfare of young people.

Merger of Cable & Wireless Telegraph Companies

In 1928, following protracted negotiations in which the firm acted on behalf of the cable companies, a merger was effected between them and the Marconi wireless telegraph group of companies, so unifying the overseas telegraphic communications of the British Empire. After World War II the merger company, Cable & Wireless Ltd., of which a former member of the staff, R. E. R. Luff, was a managing director, was acquired by the United Kingdom Government and the firm continues to audit its accounts as well as the accounts of Cable & Wireless (Holding) Ltd.—now no longer connected with telegraphs, but the largest investment trust company in Great Britain. It was awarded nearly £32 m. by an independent tribunal for its telegraphic interests, supplementing its already large resources not taken over by the State.

Opening of further offices abroad

Several offices were opened in Europe during the 1920's: Paris in 1920, Brussels and Antwerp in 1924, Rome in 1923, and Milan in 1927. In 1924, in conjunction with Binder, Hamlyn & Co., offices were established in Vienna and Berlin, under the name of Deloitte, Plender, Binder & Co., to handle mid-European business then on the upsurge, backed by large American capital. Berlin Office did not justify itself and was closed in 1927; and in view of the German occupation of Austria and the threat of war in 1938 it was decided to close Vienna Office and its sub-offices at Budapest and Prague. New York Office opened a branch at Havana, Cuba, in 1914.

Deloitte, Plender, Haskins & Sells

The close and friendly relations which exist between the firm and Haskins & Sells, one of the most prominent accounting firms in the United States, began in 1925 when the practices of the two firms in Canada (where another office was opened in Toronto in 1930), Cuba, and Mexico were combined in a co-partnership under the name of Deloitte, Plender, Haskins & Sells. In 1930 separate co-partnerships with the same title were entered into at the various places where Deloittes were established in South America and South Africa primarily to carry out engagements originating from Haskins & Sells: the resident partners in the Deloitte offices became the resident partners also in the composite firms.

British Broadcasting Corporation: Race-course Betting Control Board

The firm was appointed auditors of the newly formed British Broadcasting Corporation (as it had been of its predecessor company) and of the Race-course Betting Control Board, which was established by Act of Parliament to set up and operate totalizators. The idiosyncrasies of gambling legislation in this country are a strange commentary on the public conscience, as interpreted by Parliament. The idea of a government issue of premium bonds was discountenanced until 1956, forty-one years after Sir William Plender had advocated this means of using the sporting instincts of the public to provide funds for the national exchequer during World War I.

Depression of 1920–30: Hatry Companies collapse

At the end of the 1920's the postwar years of prosperity, both here and in the United States, turned to disillusionment. There ensued a long and grim period of acute industrial depression with severe unemployment. 'In the autumn of 1929', writes Sir Arthur Bryant in *English Saga 1840–1940*, 'a series of crashes on the New York Stock Exchange was followed by a failure of credit from one end of Europe to the other. The great world economic crisis and trade blizzard began. It was grimmer and bigger than any that had ever happened.' In *The First Fifty Years—1895–1945*, Haskins & Sells describe the American scene:

As the nation rolled down through the lush twenties a new era of easy prosperity and universal happiness seemed to have arrived. The prices of industrial shares on the stock market rose higher and higher and kept on soaring to unheard of levels. Scores of thousands of people in all walks of life discovered how to buy 100 shares of stock on margin for a price of 20 or 30 in cash and a pledge of all of it against the balance due . . . in 1929 the wildest boom in history culminated in a panic on the New York Stock Exchange.

It is a measure of the economic difficulties of the United States that in 1933 the rate of exchange dropped to $5.27 to the £, compared with the gold parity of $4.86 and the present rate of $2.80. In the United Kingdom the years 1928–9 will be remembered for the spate of company flotations in which a gullible public rushed to subscribe for speculative shares, expecting large gains which in fact had little or no prospects of realization. A sample analysis of the first accounts of companies making such issues in six months in 1928 showed that thirty-six companies, whose profits had been estimated at nearly £3½ m., suffered losses of £642,000, and that many of them had gone into liquidation. But it was the collapse in 1929 of the Hatry group of companies which shook the City and had wide repercussions in the United

Kingdom. A partner was appointed liquidator of the Parent Trust & Finance Co. Ltd., a large and once prosperous undertaking which had suffered severely in the Hatry débâcle. Hatry and others received heavy sentences for fraud and forgery and the liquidator had to interview Hatry in Maidstone Gaol to enlist his aid in unravelling some of the complicated transactions which had contributed to the downfall of the company.

Austrian Credit Anstalt

An even more far-reaching shock to the financial world was the failure of the reputable Austrian Credit Anstalt in 1931 to meet the interest on credits from foreign bankers. The resulting loss of confidence in the stability of financial institutions on the Continent was a major cause of the economic crisis in Europe. A moratorium was imposed whilst Deloitte, Plender, Binder & Co. was instructed by the foreign bankers concerned, in agreement with Credit Anstalt and the Austrian Ministry of Finance, to investigate the bank's affairs. One of the conditions of acceptance by the foreign banks of scrip in satisfaction of their claims was that the Vienna firm should be appointed auditors of the bank: and on the occupation of Austria by Hitler a representative of the firm was obliged to witness the removal of the bank's gold and foreign currencies and their replacement by German notes.

National Economy Committee

In 1931 it began to look as if the country was heading for bankruptcy and the Government set up a National Economy Committee whose urgent task was to recommend how best to curtail State expenditure. The committee of five included three accountants, of whom Sir William Plender was one—another example of the growing importance which the Government attached to the judgement of accountants in matters of State.

Royal Mail Steam Packet Company case

Of more direct and pressing importance to practising accountants at this time was the trial of the chairman and the auditor of the Royal Mail Steam Packet Company, a *cause célèbre* in the annals of modern accountancy. The chairman, Lord Kylsant, was sentenced to twelve months' imprisonment for issuing a false prospectus upon which charge he alone was prosecuted, but both he and the auditor (a respected member of a large London firm) were acquitted on the charge of issuing false accounts in which it had been alleged that losses were converted into profits by the use of internal reserves, indicated only by obscure phrases, and manifestly presenting an untrue picture of current results. On this aspect of the case the judge made the following observations:

We have heard a great deal about the keeping of secret reserves, and we have heard a great deal about the commercial troubles which may flow from that practice. We have heard a great deal about what is often done in practice, and it may be reasonably and properly done, but the question may arise someday, and possibly will arise, in some appropriate proceeding, in order to find out and elucidate these very special matters. It was said by a learned judge on one occasion, by way of observation and not by judgment, that a company, that is to say the shareholders, could not complain if the position of the finances of the company was better than the accounts disclosed. That has been quoted from time to time as a justification for this method of keeping reserves secret. But there may be very great evils if those who have the control and management of companies, and who control and manage companies for the benefit of shareholders who entrust their moneys to companies, have very large portions of the company's assets left in the secret disposition of the managing authority. It may work very well in many cases: no doubt it does. It is a practice which is being followed, no doubt, by many concerns of the highest standing. On the other hand, it may be the subject of almost intolerable abuse. Such a system may be used to cover up negligences, irregularities and almost breaches of faith. It is said to be a matter of domestic concern between the company and the shareholders, but if shareholders do not know and cannot know what the position is, how can they form any view about it at all?

The Times commented:

If there can be degrees of gravity in charges of the kind brought against two men of this pivotal value in the commercial life of the country, then the charge made against the auditor was the graver in point of public importance. If it had succeeded it must have been a heavy blow to a profession whose integrity is its life.

Evolution of Company Law and effect of Royal Mail case on profession

The Royal Mail case gave accountants a sense of increased responsibility and strengthened the authority of the auditor, morally if not legally: the absence of statutory requirements to support what an auditor considered to be desirable disclosures in published accounts placed him at a serious disadvantage, which successive Company Law Amendment Committees up to that time had done little to remove. Thus the 1918 Committee had reported:

As a commercial matter publication of profit and loss ought not to be required in the absence of very strong reason and we do not find that such reason exists. To require from a corporation a public disclosure of profit and loss which is not required from a firm or an individual gives an unfair advantage to a competitor in trade and does not commend itself to our judgment.

The Companies Act 1929 went some way towards imposing statutory obligations for more informative accounts, as recommended by a committee which reported in 1926, but the outlook of that committee would hardly have been so conservative had it reported five years later. The preamble to their report said:

The system of company law and practice in force has been gradually evolved to meet the needs of the community at large and the commercial community in particular. We consider that in general it fulfils this object in a highly satisfactory manner. We have refrained from recommending any important change which was not, in our view, quite clearly demanded and justified by the evidence before us. We realise that the system of limited liability leaves opportunities for abuse. Some of these we consider part of the price which the community has to pay for the adoption of a system so beneficial to its trade and industry.

It was left to the Institute of Chartered Accountants in England and Wales to urge upon their members the application of standards of the best practice, and these were substantially enacted in the Companies Act of 1948, as recommended by the Cohen Committee of 1943. A preamble of their report stated:

The present legal requirements as to the contents of the accounts to be presented to shareholders are too meagre. The practice of showing a number of diverse items in one lump sum and thereby obscuring the real position as to the assets and liabilities, and as to the results of trading, makes it difficult and often impossible for a shareholder to form a true view of the financial position and earnings of the company in which he is interested. While auditors have tended to press for standards in advance of the requirements of the present law, it has been suggested that their hands would be strengthened if the law were to accord more nearly with what they regard as the best practice.

The obligation upon the auditor to state whether accounts are not only true but fair, as opposed to true and correct previously, has decisively widened his influence and responsibility. The London Stock Exchange, through its regulations and requirements for granting quotations, has also been a potent means of protecting shareholders and the public.

Sir William Plender again elected president of Institute

Sir William Plender, who had been created a baronet in 1923, was again elected president of the Institute, this time for the Jubilee year 1929–30, and presided at a banquet in the Guildhall to commemorate the fiftieth anniversary since the granting of the Royal Charter. He laid the foundation stone of the considerable extension of the Institute building in Moorgate Place. In 1929, accompanied by Russell Kettle, he attended the third International Congress of Accounting in New York and delivered a paper on 'Depreciation and Obsolescence from the viewpoint of the investor in securities.' At the previous congress in Amsterdam in 1926 he had read a paper on 'The Accountant's certificate in connection with the Accountant's responsibility.' He was elected president of the fourth International Congress, held in London in 1933, when he entertained the Congress members at a garden party at his country home in Kent. At that congress Arthur Cutforth read a paper on 'Exchange Fluctuations in relation to Accounting as regards operating results and asset values.' When Lord Plender died in 1946 he had been a member of the council for forty-three years and chairman of the Parliamentary and Law Committee from 1913 to 1931. His portrait by Sir William

Llewellyn, P.R.A., hangs in the Oak Hall at the Institute, a fitting memorial to one to whom the profession owes much.

Sir William's public services between the wars

During the years between the wars, Sir William, who had become Baron Plender of Sundridge in the county of Kent in 1930, continued to interest himself not only in his active professional life but also in the affairs of the Institute and in public service to the nation. When in 1927 the honorary degree of LL.D. was conferred upon him by Birmingham University, the Vice-Chancellor said:

The list of Sir William's public and professional services is impressive by its variety and its range: a schedule of the Commissions, Royal, Departmental and Industrial, on which he has sat would require for accuracy an auditor's certificate.

To his services during the 1914–18 war, already enumerated, he added the chairmanship of the National Board for the Coal Industry, of the Ministry of Labour Grants Committee, of the Advisory Committee of the Trade Facilities Act, of the Enemy Debts Clearing Office, and of the German Debts Committee. He was a member of committees and other bodies dealing with the office organization of the Public Trustee; London Cross River Traffic; Church of England Finances; Export Credits; the Lord Chancellor's Committee on the Remuneration of Solicitors; the Iron and Steel Committee of the Economic Advisory Council; Tribunal on Ministry of Munitions; Tribunal on Coal Mining Royalties; and Railway Amalgamations Tribunal. His versatility and breadth of vision in other spheres were remarkable and the many speeches and addresses he gave were notable for felicity of language. His life was clouded by a tragedy when at the height of his career Lady Plender died on 31 December 1930, the day before the announcement of his peerage in the New Year's Honours List.

Knighthood conferred on Alan Rae Smith

In 1935 Alan Rae Smith was knighted in recognition of his services as a member of the Colonial Development Advisory Committee of which he was chairman from 1935 to 1940.

Death of P. D. Griffiths

In 1937 Percival D. Griffiths, known to many generations of those who passed through Deloittes as P. D., was thrown from his horse and killed at the age of 75 while hunting with the Whaddon Chase. The wish he had so often expressed to die in the saddle was granted. He was known to a wide circle of clients and friends as a delightful personality; but he did not seek professional eminence and was content for the most part to relieve his partners of much of the internal administration work of the office. His chief interest in life was his famous collection of antique furniture. How he came to acquire this collection has been told by Mr. R. W. Symonds in an article in *Country Life* of 13 June 1952, from which the following is taken:

He was fortunate with his first purchase, for it was a genuine and well-designed bureau bookcase made about 1740; but he was not so lucky with later purchases, almost all of which, for a time, were spurious, in spite of their having been mistakenly praised in articles written by authorities on furniture.

His discovery that his collection of furniture was rather less than antique was made in circumstances not undramatic. One day in about 1910 he saw by chance in a window of a shop in a London back street a mahogany tripod table, with a richly carved stem and legs, identical with one he had recently bought. He was somewhat puzzled at this, for he considered his table to be a rare example of Chippendale's best work. He entered the shop and asked the shopkeeper its price. To his surprise and annoyance he was told that it was a hundred pounds less than he had paid for his tripod table.

They were soon talking about the beauty of old craftsmanship, which, Griffiths observed, was lost today. The eyes of the shopkeeper twinkled: 'It's not all that lost' he said. 'Let me tell you, sir, that I made this table.' He leaned toward Griffiths and said in a lowered and confidential tone of voice: 'And what's more I've made in the last few years a large number of such pieces of Chippendale for an old buffer who lives at St. Albans!'

'How very interesting' said Percival Griffiths, already envisaging the letter his lawyers would be writing to the dealer who had sold him his tripod table and many other pieces in his collection. In due course the Griffiths collection of choice fakes was piled into a van and returned.

After such an experience, another collector would have had enough of antique furniture; but not Percival Griffiths. He now began, but with much more caution, to make a collection of walnut and mahogany furniture which became, by the time he died in 1937, the finest collection in the country.

Griffiths loved not only 18th-century furniture, but also the 18th-century way of life. His house, Sandridgebury, was once an old farmhouse, which he had enlarged and converted, but not modernised, for it was illuminated by oil-lamps and candles and the only heating was from open wood fires. The bathrooms had japanned baths with their polished mahogany surrounds dating from Victorian times. His bed was a four-poster with yellow curtains for summer time and red for winter.

125

The firm suffered a heavy loss in 1938 by the retirement through ill-health, at the age of 57, of Arthur Cutforth. He had been knighted earlier in that year in recognition of his many public services. He had been the chairman of the Reorganization Committee for Milk for Great Britain, a member of the Food Council, of the Oil from Coal sub-committee of the Committee of Imperial Defence, of the Tithe Redemption Commission, and Accountant Assessor to the Royal Commission on the Coal Industry. He was High Sheriff of Hertfordshire in 1937–8. Sir Arthur was president of the Institute of Chartered Accountants during the two years 1934–6, and throughout his active life was assiduous in furthering the interests of the profession. His many writings and his addresses to members of the Institute and other bodies, particularly to students, were notable for their lucidity and the ease with which practice and theory were harmonized. His books, *Methods of Amalgamation and the Valuation of Businesses* and *Audits*, are still standard works. The staff at London Wall Buildings owed much to his thought for their welfare. Perhaps more than any other partner in the period of the firm's expansion between the wars he foresaw the need of improvements in organization. His brilliant mind and engaging personality contributed much to the increase in the practice during his twenty-seven years as a partner. In his retirement he wrote a small volume of *Random Reminiscences* of some of the lighter episodes in his business life. Sir Harold Howitt, G.B.E., D.S.O., M.C., F.C.A., wrote in a preface:

To recent members of the Institute and to students, he is perhaps chiefly known as the author of various books and papers, but these only represent one side of his activities and of his interest in the profession and in young people. To those who had the joy of knowing him in active work, and as a friend, he stood for very much more. He stood for all that was best in professional life, in ability, in playing the game, in helpfulness and in a Puckish sense of humour.

Russell Kettle was appointed a member of the Tithe Redemption Commission on the resignation of Sir Arthur Cutforth.

Scholastic appointments

In 1939 a partner was appointed as auditor of the accounts of the University of Oxford. These are commonly called 'The Chest', and an ancient chest in which moneys and valuables of the University were deposited under lock and key is still to be seen in the Secretary's office. Other scholastic appointments of the firm include the audits of Eton, Harrow, and Rugby schools.

Gaumont-British Picture Corporation Ltd.

An engagement of unusual interest which attracted much publicity arose from the dissatisfaction of a large number of shareholders in the Gaumont-British Picture Corporation with the conduct of the company's affairs and the paucity of information supplied to them which had been the subject of protracted agitation. It culminated in 1939 in the appointment by the Board of Trade of a partner in the firm as Inspector to investigate the allegations and report on their validity. The structure of the corporation, with its large group of subsidiary and associated companies, made the inquiry difficult and complicated. Eventually disputes as to the legal rights of an inspector to require information relating to the underlying companies created difficulties which proved insurmountable in the then state of the law. After the Inspector had completed the inquiry as far as was practicable he arranged to exercise his power to examine the managing director on oath. The managing director declined, however, to answer questions in the presence of a shorthand writer employed by the Inspector to make a note of the proceedings. The situation thus created made it impossible for the Inspector to carry out his duties effectively and after protesting he withdrew and reported the matter to the Court. The Court held that the refusal to comply with the requirement of the Inspector, as an officer of the Court, was not justified and was tantamount to contempt. At this crucial point the war broke out; the inquiry was postponed *sine die* and the parties to it ultimately composed their differences.

Plans for carrying on business in war-time

As international tension grew and the outbreak of World War II seemed inevitable, the firm made preparations for carrying on the practice if hostilities ensued. The view was commonly held that a heavy air attack aimed as a knock-out blow at London was probable as soon as war was declared, and that the contingency of being unable to carry on business from the City should be provided for. A plan was evolved for the grouping of staff around London according to the location of their homes, and for partners and senior clerks to control their sections by telephone. As a precaution it was arranged that staff should disperse and avoid coming to the office for the first three days of the war. Fears of early attack were, however, unjustified and the staff resumed attendance at 5, London Wall Buildings after the three-day interval. A property was, however, rented at Caterham in Surrey to house the Taxation Department, whose work was likely to grow in volume and importance, and the staff concerned found living accommodation in the neighbourhood. Although the Caterham office escaped damage, the choice of that district for safety against air raids did not turn out eventually to be a good one as it proved to be in the path of a great many of the raiders. The partners persuaded Lord Plender, then approaching 79 years of age, to leave London and except for an occasional visit to the office, he spent the war years at Torquay: his London and country houses were both rendered uninhabitable by bomb damage and much of his collection of old furniture and *objets d'art* was badly damaged. Sir Alan Rae Smith was a member of a conference hastily called by the Government to consider the possibility of instituting a scheme of insurance for war damage to fixed property.

Effect of World War II on the office

The firm had encouraged members of the staff to join the Territorial Army and sixty-six men were immediately called up for military service: this loss, mainly of qualified and experienced accountants, was much heavier than would appear in relation to the total staff of 351 of all grades and both sexes. Although the liability to military service of qualified accountants upon reaching a certain age was deferred, they were liable to be directed into the service of government departments where specialized accounting experience was in great demand. The depleted permanent staff who remained were assisted by a fluctuating temporary staff recruited from persons under or over military age of both sexes. In all, 144 men joined the Forces and, as already stated, twenty-four lost their lives. Those who remained mostly joined auxiliary services such as the Home Guard and Civil Defence which involved much all-night work during which two members of the staff were killed. A look-out post on the roof of 5, London Wall Buildings was manned, from which warning signals were passed to the office on the approach of enemy raiders; and an all-night service of fire-watching was instituted. The constant interruptions by air raids made serious inroads into the time of partners and staff and the organization of the firm's work was further impeded by the evacuation to the country of the offices of many clients whose own depleted staffs threw a further burden on the auditors. Looking back, the period of the war seems like a nightmare. The firm has much reason to be grateful to the staff for the way in which they carried on, often under almost insuperable difficulties and danger. During the sixty-seven nights of continuous air raids in 1940–1, and later during intermittent air raids, and in 1944 and 1945 when the enemy used flying bombs and rockets, the railways into London were severely damaged and the main line termini often rendered unusable for weeks on end. Travelling by circuitous routes to and from the City, often after a sleepless night, occupied a con-siderable part of the day and air raid warnings interrupted the limited working hours. Those who succeeded by devious means in reaching the City on the morning of 11 May 1941 will carry throughout their lives a vivid recollection of the effects of the tragic events of the previous night. Sir Winston Churchill in the third volume of his *War Memories* says:

On May 10 the enemy returned to London with incendiary bombs.

He lit more than two thousand fires and, by the smashing of nearly a hundred and fifty water mains, coupled with the low tide in the Thames, he stopped us putting them out. At six o'clock next morning hundreds were reported as out of control and four were still alight on the night of the 13th. It was the most destructive attack of the whole night Blitz. Five docks and seventy-one key points, half of which were factories, had been lit. All but one of the main railway stations were blocked for weeks, and the through routes were not fully opened till early June. Over three thousand people were killed or injured. In other respects it was also historic. It destroyed the House of Commons. This, though we did not know it, was the enemy's parting fling.

A large area not far from the office was razed to the ground, but the office itself miraculously escaped serious damage although the rest of London Wall Buildings was almost wholly gutted by fire. The store-rooms in the basement containing most of the firm's old papers and documents were flooded, and it is small wonder that in the midst of so much destruction few of the firm's old records survived. Other accommodation fortunately was available in Lombard Street and the firm was housed there for a fortnight until it was possible to return to 5, London Wall Buildings to engage in an orgy of clearing up. Swansea Office was completely destroyed. After Hitler's invasion of the Low Countries and France, the partners and most of the British staff in Paris and Brussels Offices managed to escape to the United Kingdom, often after terrifying experiences. The Italian offices were closed in anticipation of the entry of Italy into the war.

Special work during World War II

The demands on the profession during the war were stretched to the full. Not only had practitioners to cope with much of their

131

normal peace-time work, often in circumstances of extreme difficulty, but their services were invoked to a greater degree than in World War I to assist the authorities in the application of restrictions and regulations over a wide range of activities. Examples were price and quantity controls, costing of contracts, limitation of profits, and compensation claims. Income tax stood at 10s. in the £, with an additional 9s. 6d. surtax in the top range of incomes. An excess profits duty of 20s. in the £ was levied. The Taxation Department was overworked. A minor embarrassment was the severe shortage of paper and many expedients were resorted to in order to conserve supplies.

The firm was again entrusted with the winding up of the London branches of enemy banks, consisting this time of two Italian banks (Banca Commerciale Italiana and Credito Italiano) and two Japanese banks (the Yokohama Specie Bank and the Bank of Taiwan). Other work included the giving of advice and evidence on the amount of compensation to be paid by British interests for the acquisition of enemy businesses, and by the Government itself for companies compulsorily taken over. These included a large aircraft factory whose management and output during the war were regarded as unsatisfactory and a company which owned and exercised sovereign powers over an important Eastern territory. Russell Kettle was a member of the Joint Stores Committee of the British Red Cross and St. John War Organization and the only accountancy representative on the Companies Act Amendment Committee set up in 1943 by the Government, and known as the Cohen Committee, to formulate suggestions in readiness for bringing the law into line with modern requirements as soon as possible after the restoration of peace. The appointment of this committee in the middle of the war has been described by Mr. Nicholas A. H. Stacey in *English Accountancy 1800–1954* as a singularly imaginative action and an example of much foresight on the part of a government which already had its hands full. Sir Alan Rae Smith served as Financial Adviser to the Ministry of Shipping (later Ministry of Transport) and on numerous affiliated committees dealing with various aspects of shipping and other forms of transport. For these services he was created Knight Commander of the Order of the British Empire in 1948. He was also nominated by the Government to serve as a member of the Arbitration Tribunal to determine the sum payable to Courtaulds Ltd. for shares in their important American subsidiary, compulsorily acquired by H.M. Treasury for sale to American interests.

Two additional partners, Frank A. Lord and John Godfrey, were admitted in 1942. They had both been senior members of the staff for many years. J. W. Baird retired in the same year.

Economic changes following World War II

The transition from war to peace brought in its train many new problems affecting the internal and external economy of the United Kingdom. The postwar Government embarked upon a policy of nationalization and within the four years 1946–9 the State took over the Bank of England, the Coal Mines, the Railways, the Electricity and Gas Industries, and the Steel Industry. S. J. L. Hardie, a former member of Deloittes' staff, was appointed chairman of the National Steel Board; but after completion of the scheme a succeeding government denationalized the industry. Another former member of the staff, D. H. Cameron of Lochiel, T.D., who was articled to the firm, is a member of the British Transport Commission. The services of many chartered accountants, including members of the firm, were used by the Government and clients in connexion with the determination of compensation for the acquisition of nationalized undertakings. Sir Russell Kettle, as he later became, was a member of the Railways Arbitration Tribunal established to award compensation for railways and canals for which the purchase price could not be related to Stock Exchange quotations. The concentration in big nationalized units of industries previously carried on through large numbers of public and private companies meant the loss of a number of old and valued clients, but a member of the firm was appointed joint auditor of the British Transport Commission and the firm was appointed auditors of the London Electricity Board and the South Eastern Gas Board. The firm also received the appointment of auditors to the National Dock Labour Board, in the formation of which Sir Alan Rae Smith had acted as Financial Adviser.

Death of Lord Plender

On 19 January 1946 Lord Plender died at the age of 84. He was the last survivor of the outstanding triumvirate whose names figure in the title of the firm, and who between them had guided its destinies for over a century. On the previous 5 December Lord Plender had sent a signed message to the office in which he said:

It is a great disappointment to me to be absent from the firm during this, the centenary year of its existence, and I thought I would like to send a message to those at 5, London Wall Buildings before the close of this memorable year.

Part of a large area near London Wall Buildings destroyed in air-raid, 1940

(By permission of the Director, Guildhall Art Gallery)

For some years I have been senior partner in the firm and I could not have had more devoted colleagues and friends during that period, and through the very many years preceding it when I was a junior partner and a member of the staff.

As I sit quietly in a nursing home my thoughts turn to the many devoted friends I made and those memories brighten my declining years. I have much to be thankful for and I owe almost everything in life to the firm and to the opportunities given me there. I can never revisit London but memories remain and they centre round the old firm of which I am very proud. Long may it flourish after its centenary this year.

Lord Plender's funeral took place at St. Mary's church, Sundridge, and a memorial service was held at St. Margaret's, Westminster. There were many tributes in the national press and in letters to the firm, many of them from societies and organizations with which he had been connected. *The Accountant* referred to him as the outstanding figure in the world of accountancy, with an international reputation, and said it would be hard to exaggerate the contribution he made towards building up and consolidating the profession. *The Times* emphasized his public and other services to the nation and the community:

Throughout his career he served his country with untiring zeal, his services being particularly valuable during the 1914–1918 war and the years which came after it, when the skill of accountants was specially in demand. Whenever it was a question of figures and their meaning, his sane and sober counsel was available and his high reputation for solid common sense and sterling honesty gave weight to his opinions and decisions. . . . His unfailing readiness for steady patient work made him invaluable to his country. . . . Never flustered or irritated at a time when the nerves of so many good workers were on edge, Plender was one of the figures that made all with whom he came into contact feel

135

that victory was assured to a country that had such imperturbable advisers.

After enumerating 'his amazing list of activities in the 1914–1918 war and after the war period', to which reference has already been made, *The Times* catalogued many of his other offices and honours; High Sheriff of the County of London, 1927–8, and of Kent, 1928–9; Lieutenant of the City of London and Deputy Lieutenant of the County of London; Knight Justice of the Order of St. John of Jerusalem; honorary member of the Institute of Journalists and of the Institution of Civil Engineers; honorary treasurer of the Royal Society of Painter-Etchers and Engravers; vice-president of the Poplar Hospital for Accidents; governor of St. Thomas's Hospital; president of Kent County Cricket Club; chairman, and later president, of the governing body of the City of London College; and governor of Kings School, Canterbury. He is remembered by many, young and old, for his humanity, kindliness, and tolerance to those seeking his advice or in need of practical help to reinstate themselves in life after misfortune had overtaken them. A reference recently in the press to a Plender Street in St. Pancras led to the discovery that it was so named at the suggestion of a man to whom Lord Plender had given a helping hand, and who later became a member of the London County Council.

Further changes in partnership

Staff shortage continued to be a major embarrassment for some time after the war, but the firm's business expanded and between 1946 and 1957 twelve additional partners were admitted: Wilfrid Guy Densem and Laurence John Culshaw in

1946; Robert T. M. McPhail in 1947; Arnold Wilfred Sarson in 1948; Vernon A. Tudball and Charles Romer-Lee in 1949; Gordon E. Morrish in 1950; Ronald F. George in 1952; David D. Rae Smith (son of Sir Alan Rae Smith) and Stanley P. Wilkins in 1954; and J. Ness Prentice and Richard Kettle (son of Sir Russell Kettle) in 1957. Two partners were nominated by the Council of the Institute of Chartered Accountants to act as examiners, and subsequently as moderators, in the final qualifying examinations, and Guy Densem was on several occasions a group leader at the Institute's Summer School at Christ Church, Oxford, where he delivered an address in 1950 on the subject, then topical, of the new Companies Act. Wilfred Sarson undertook, with a member of the Bar, the task of editing a new edition of the standard work *Kerr on Receivers*. Harold Hockley, an accountant of outstanding ability, retired in 1950 at the age of 60 and James Kilpatrick, who had he not employed his talents in the accountancy profession would have made his mark as a man of letters, was obliged to retire by ill health in 1953 at the age of 64.

Death of Harold Read

January 1947 brought another severe blow to the firm by the sudden death of Harold Read at the age of 61. He was of a modest and retiring disposition yet possessed of a dry sense of humour. Extremely popular with clients, his clear and incisive analysis of financial problems and his skill in their practical solution was based upon a fair and equitable consideration of the interests of all parties. In particular he possessed a wide knowledge and experience of the accounting problems of banks, banking institutions, and utility undertakings. *The Times* stated in a brief obituary notice:

Mr. Read was a very shrewd accountant with versatile interests and was well liked by all with whom he came in contact in the City and elsewhere.

He was fond of sport and, like A. R. Hollebone eighty years previously, hunted with the Old Surrey.

New Companies Act 1948

In 1948 company accounts took on a new look, and the resources of the firm were fully occupied in translating into practice the many detailed requirements of the new Companies Act. Sir Russell Kettle had received the honour of Knighthood in 1947 in recognition of his work as a member of the Cohen Committee on Company Law Amendment and for advising the Government on the implementation of the committee's accounting recommendations in the new Act of Parliament. He delivered an address at the autumnal meeting of the Institute of Chartered Accountants in 1947 on the accounts and audit provisions of the new Act. No longer was it possible to invoke the necessity of withholding information from competitors as a reason for depriving shareholders of a true and fair statement of accounts. The lessons of the Royal Mail case had been learned and applied.

Manchester and Truro Offices

In 1949 an office was opened in Manchester with Douglas R. Fendick as resident partner, in order to handle the growing volume of work in the north-west which had required a resident staff in Manchester for some years previously. It has been the firm's policy to open provincial offices only when the volume of existing business in the district justified doing so as a matter of business convenience. A small office opened in Truro in 1920 was discontinued in 1945.

Sir Russell Kettle elected president of the Institute

Sir Russell Kettle was appointed president of the Institute for 1949–50 and was the fifth member of the firm to occupy that position. During and after World War II the ever-widening scope and enhanced prestige of the profession had brought the Institute into greater prominence as the premier body of accountants in the United Kingdom and this placed a much greater burden than hitherto upon the members of the council. The office of president had become an almost whole-time job and involved much travelling to visit and address the numerous district societies and many of the students' societies. The lunches and dinners attended by the president on these occasions, and similar functions of kindred societies and official bodies of various kinds, were legion. At the conclusion of his year of office, the president was the recipient of a handsome silver inkstand on which was inscribed:

Presented to Sir Russell Kettle by senior members of the staff of Deloitte, Plender, Griffiths & Co., as a token of their esteem and to mark his year of office as President of the Institute of Chartered Accountants 1949–1950.

The partners and their wives gave a dinner at Claridges to Sir Russell and Lady Kettle, at which the managers and their wives were also present, to celebrate his year of office.

Gezira Cotton Board

In 1950 the firm was appointed by the Sudan Government to act as auditors of the Sudan Gezira Board and since the Sudan achieved independence this appointment has been renewed annually by the Sudanese Minister of Finance and Economics. The Gezira Board, a non-profit-making government corporation, supervises the growing of cotton by native cultivators, the picking of the cotton, its delivery to the board's ginning factories, and its eventual sale, accounting to each cultivator for his share of the produce from the irrigated land let to him. The vast cotton industry is the major factor in the economy of the Sudan; and the audit takes several assistants to the tropical heat of the Sudan for some months each year. Up to the formation of the board the operations had been carried out under concession by a private company, whose accounts had been periodically examined by the firm since 1925 on behalf of the Sudan Government, to confirm its share of results.

Closer association with Haskins & Sells

In the year 1952 there was a development of major importance in the firm's North American business. Of the British firms which had started to practise in the United States at the turn of the century before the profession in America was organized, Deloittes alone had retained control of its American business from London; and it was felt that the premier place and influence the United States had gained in world economy called for a new assessment of the firm's policy in the New World. To maintain and expand the business in a continent the size of North

America called for a network of branches at the main centres of industry. This inevitably involved considerable numbers of partners and qualified staff, as well as substantial capital commitments. Furthermore, organization must be essentially American in character. Following conversations in London and New York with Arthur B. Foye and Weldon Powell of Haskins & Sells it was agreed that the businesses of Deloittes and Haskins & Sells in the United States, where the latter firm had thirty-four offices, should be merged and carried on under the name of Haskins & Sells, and that some of the partners in London, as representing the interests of Deloittes, should in future be partners in Haskins & Sells. The resident partners of Deloittes in the United States became partners in Haskins & Sells. It was also agreed to form separate composite partnerships of Deloitte, Plender, Haskins & Sells at each place where the business of Haskins & Sells was carried on in the United States, to deal with work performed for Deloitte clients resident outside the United States. The business of Haskins & Sells in London and Paris and in certain other places outside the United States was in future to be undertaken by new composite firms of Deloitte, Plender, Haskins & Sells. Composite firms have since been formed in Puerto Rico at San Juan, in Colombia at Medellin and Bogota, in Venezuela at Caracas, and in Japan at Tokyo. The organization of Deloitte, Plender, Haskins & Sells in Canada has been considerably expanded, mainly by mergers with firms of Canadian chartered accountants. The first of these mergers was with the well-known firm of Millar Macdonald & Co. of Winnipeg. Thereafter, mergers took place with Paisley, Wallace & Co. of Vancouver and Prince George, Rooke, Thomas & Co. of Regina,

Patriquin, Duncan, McClary, McClary & Co. of Edmonton and Calgary, and Macdonald & Healy of Windsor.

The London partners in the firm of Haskins & Sells keep in close touch with the American partners and attend the annual conferences of the partners in that firm, held for three days at a country club within easy distance of New York. Here current topics of professional and domestic interest are discussed. At the gathering in 1954 Arthur B. Foye, the head of the American firm, drew attention to the fact that there were present the president of the American Institute (himself), the president of the Canadian Institute (Walter Macdonald, the senior resident partner of the composite firm in Canada), and a past president of the English Institute (Sir Russell Kettle).

Australian firm

The growing need to provide an organization in Australia to handle the work of British clients in that continent led to the formation in 1953 of an Australian firm of Deloitte, Plender, Griffiths & Co. in Sydney and Melbourne, in which some of the members of the firms of Yarwood Vane & Co. of Sydney and W. H. Tuckett & Sons of Melbourne joined members of the London firm as partners.

In recent years there has been a resumption of the exchange of visits, interrupted by the war, between partners in the London and overseas firms, including the Australian firm.

Retirement of Sir Russell Kettle

On 31 March 1955 Sir Russell Kettle retired at the age of 68, at the same time resigning his seat on the council of the Institute, and the chairmanship of the Accountants Advisory Committee on the Companies Act appointed by the Board of Trade. At the firm's annual dinner and dance in the previous October there was a pleasant interlude when the staff presented an antique clock to Sir Russell on the completion of fifty years' service with the firm.

Special engagements in West Africa

The firm was engaged during 1956 on two unusual inquiries which attracted much publicity by reason of their political implications. At the request of the Colonial Office a partner was nominated to serve on a Commission at Accra appointed by the Government of the Gold Coast (now Ghana) to inquire into the affairs of the Gold Coast Cocoa Purchasing Co. Ltd. in connexion with allegations reflecting on the Government. Another partner travelled to Nigeria at the request of the Colonial Office to investigate the affairs of a local bank, in connexion with which improprieties were alleged, reflecting upon members of one of the regional governments.

Retirement of Sir Alan Rae Smith

Sir Alan Rae Smith retired at the age of 71 on 30 September 1956. During his partnership his ability had been particularly in evidence in the many successful business negotiations he had conducted on behalf of clients. His able and shrewd assessment of practical possibilities in solving difficult problems was well known. Apart from his valuable services to the country, already mentioned, he advised the Home Secretary on the revisions of London taxicab fares in 1950 and 1951 and was a member of the Taxicab Committee in 1952. He continues to act as honorary

143

treasurer of the Royal Institute of International Affairs and since his retirement has joined the boards of some of the firm's clients.

Portraits of former partners

The portraits of past partners hang in the main corridor at 5, London Wall Buildings. It is to be feared that they are sometimes referred to irreverently as the Rogues Gallery! Photographs of the three great figures of the past, Deloitte, Plender, and John Griffiths, are prominently displayed in the reception office.

W. G. Densem and R. T. M. McPhail as senior partners

On the retirement of Sir Alan Rae Smith the leadership of the firm passed to W. G. Densem and R. T. M. McPhail as joint senior partners. Mr. Densem, who had for some time taken an active part in the affairs of the Institute, was elected to fill the vacancy on the council caused by the resignation of Sir Russell Kettle.

Retrospect 1901–56

In the half-century which has passed since the firm moved to 5, London Wall Buildings the number of partners in the United Kingdom has risen from six to nineteen and the staff has increased from 125 to 578. The office has been enlarged on several occasions to provide adequate and more up-to-date accommodation and facilities. Specialization has called for greater segregation of activities into departments. Expansion of the firm's overseas practice has added forty offices to the solitary branch at New York in 1900, apart from the numerous affiliated offices carried on in association with Haskins & Sells.

Between 1900 and 1955 the number of limited companies in-corporated in Great Britain rose from 29,730 with a nominal capital of £1,622 m. to 291,153 with a nominal capital of £6,811 m. The nominal amount of securities quoted on the London Stock Exchange, including home and foreign government loans and overseas undertakings, increased from £8,358 m. to £27,749 m. The measure of the country's financial sacrifices in two World Wars, including their inflationary effect on its economy, is illustrated by the rise in the National Debt from £639 m. to over £27,000 m. and in the annual government expenditure, apart from local government expenditure, from £144 m. to £4,500 m. During this period of fifty-five years membership of the Institute of Chartered Accountants in England and Wales increased from 2,623 to nearly 19,000 and other bodies of accountants then in existence or established subsequently have added substantially to their members.

Some former members of the staff who have gained distinction

Apart from those members of the staff who have devoted their professional lives and talents to the firm, many have left to practice on their own account. Many others have passed through the office to gain some experience of business life before embark-ing on varied careers and in numerous cases have attained dis-tinction in the world of politics and public service, finance, and industry. Some have already been referred to: it is impracticable to name all the others, but we may mention Lord Salisbury (then Viscount Cranborne), a former Lord President of the Council and member of the Cabinet; Lord de l'Isle, V.C. (then William Philip Sydney), who was articled to the firm and has been

Secretary of State for Air; Lord Knollys (then the Hon. E. G. Knollys), a former Governor and Commander-in-Chief of Bermuda, chairman of Vickers Ltd., clients of the firm; Lord Halsbury (then Viscount Tiverton), managing director of the government-sponsored National Research Development Corporation; the Hon. Mr. Justice Stable, one of Her Majesty's Judges of the High Court; and the late Sir Charles Stewart, the first Public Trustee. And as Dickens has been twice mentioned, it is of interest to note that one of his grandsons, Philip Dickens, called 'Pip' after his namesake in *Great Expectations*, was a member of the staff for some years at 5, London Wall Buildings.

The past and the future

A few years ago the firm felt it might help new members of the staff to feel they were part of the firm's organization if they were told a little about the firm's origin, achievements, and ideals. The partners trust they will not be thought lacking in modesty or that their pride in the firm is unjustified if this story concludes with a quotation from the note prepared for this purpose:

Throughout its history the name of Deloittes has been associated by clients, the accountancy profession and the public, with the highest standard of professional competence, and known for integrity and independence. It is true to say that Deloittes has become an institution— something in the nature of an Alma Mater. No reputation can, however, rest solely upon tradition and past achievement. Everyone connected with the firm in whatever capacity has in some measure its good name in his hands. The firm has always relied upon the good sense and honour of the staff to carry out efficiently and conscientiously the duties entrusted to them and has been fortunate in the loyalty of those who serve it. It is to be hoped that the spirit which has animated past and present generations of those 'with Deloittes' will long continue.

OTHER OFFICES OF
Deloitte & Co.

AND ASSOCIATED DELOITTE FIRMS AND
THEIR RESIDENT PARTNERS

England and Wales

DELOITTE & HALLIDAY

MANCHESTER. ?–1877

James Halliday · · · · · · ?–1877

DELOITTE, PLENDER, GRIFFITHS & CO.

CARDIFF. 1912

Francis W. Higgison	1912–20
Leonard D. Williams	1920–7
Bernard E. Brown	1926–
William R. Graves	1927–53
Graeme M. Metcalf (*see Swansea*)	1953–

TRURO. 1920–45

SWANSEA. 1923

Noel T. Summerscale (*see Paris*)	1940–6
Graeme M. Metcalf (*see Cardiff*)	1950–3
David F. Pratten	1955–

MANCHESTER. 1949

Douglas R. Fendick · · · · · · 1949–

DELOITTE, PLENDER, HASKINS & SELLS

LONDON. 1952

Sir Russell Kettle	1952–5
Sir Alan Rae Smith, K.B.E.	1952–6

LONDON. 1952 *(cont.)*

Laurence J. Culshaw	1952–
Vernon A. Tudball	1952–
Stanley P. Wilkins	1954–
W. Guy Densem	1955–
Robert T. M. McPhail	1956–

Continental Europe

DELOITTE, PLENDER, GRIFFITHS & CO.	1920–
and	
DELOITTE, PLENDER, HASKINS & SELLS	1952–

FRANCE

PARIS. 1920

Edmund Heisch	1920–34
Christopher G. Coates	1920–39
George S. Murray	1923–39
Harry R. Gilbert	1934–
Noel T. Summerscale *(see Swansea)*	1940–
J. Rollo Reid	1953–

BELGIUM

BRUSSELS AND ANTWERP. 1924

Murray G. Baillie	1924–7
E. Norman Lowe	1924–55
Edward A. McGeachy	1953–

DELOITTE, PLENDER, GRIFFITHS & CO.

ITALY

ROME. 1923–36

MILAN. 1927

From 1940 to 1946 Paris, Brussels, and Antwerp Offices, and to 1949 Milan Office, were closed owing to World War II; during these periods Mr. Gilbert (who became an advisory partner resident in London in 1955) and Mr. Lowe were attached to London Office and Mr. Summerscale was a partner at Swansea Office.

PLENDER, GRIFFITHS, WYATT & CO.

RUSSIA. 1913–17
ST. PETERSBURG AND MOSCOW

Stanley C. Wyatt	1913–17

DELOITTE, PLENDER, BINDER & CO.

CENTRAL EUROPE. 1926–38
VIENNA, BERLIN, BUDAPEST, AND PRAGUE

Wallis D. Hooper	1926–8
William H. Lawson, C.B.E.	1928–30
Geoffrey H. Walsh	1930–8

North America

DELOITTE, DEVER, GRIFFITHS & CO.	1890–1905
DELOITTE, PLENDER, GRIFFITHS & CO.	1905–52

UNITED STATES OF AMERICA

NEW YORK. 1890–1952

Edward Adams	1898–1905
Francis F. White	1905–21
Frederick P. Page	1905–20
Robert L. Cuthbert	1905–11
Thomas R. Clark	1905–18
Vivian Harcourt (*see Montreal*)	1918–38
John A. Corben	1920–9
John S. Snelham	1920–9
Harold B. Atkins	1920–8
George Cochrane* (*see Havana*)	1921–52

President of the New York State Society of Certified Public Accountants 1949–50; Vice-President of the American Institute of Accountants 1941–2.

William Eyre* (*see Havana*)	1927–52
James Anderson*	1931–52
Eric K. Ernest*	1937–52
William R. McNamara*	1937–52
Monteath Ruston	1937–42
John F. Parnaby*	1942–52

* Became partners in Haskins & Sells.

149

CINCINNATI. 1905–11
        1942–52
    Vivian Harcourt (*see Mexico City*)   1905–11
    Oliver W. Seifert*   1945–52
        President of the Ohio Society of Certified Public Accountants
        1948–9.
CHICAGO. In 1890's
        1912–18
        1934–52
    James P. Macgregor   1912–18
BOSTON. 1930–52
LOS ANGELES. 1945–52

DELOITTE, PLENDER, HASKINS & SELLS   1952–

UNITED STATES OF AMERICA

NEW YORK, ATLANTA, BALTIMORE, BIRMINGHAM, BOSTON, BUFFALO, CHAR-
LOTTE, CHICAGO, CINCINNATI, CLEVELAND, DALLAS, DENVER, DETROIT,
HONOLULU, HOUSTON, JACKSONVILLE, KANSAS CITY, LOS ANGELES, MIL-
WAUKEE, MINNEAPOLIS, NEWARK, NEW HAVEN, NEW ORLEANS, OMAHA,
PHILADELPHIA, PITTSBURG, PORTLAND, ROCHESTER, SAINT LOUIS, SAN
DIEGO, SAN FRANCISCO, SEATTLE, TULSA, WASHINGTON.

Partners resident in New York

    Arthur B. Foye   1952–
        President of the American Institute of Certified Public Account-
        ants 1953–4; President of the New York State Society of
        Certified Public Accountants 1956–7.
    John W. Queenan   1952–
    Weldon Powell   1952–
    Percy R. Everett   1952–6
    J. Harry Williams   1956–

DELOITTE, PLENDER, GRIFFITHS & CO.   1912–25
DELOITTE, PLENDER, HASKINS & SELLS   1925–

CANADA

CANADIAN HEAD OFFICE. 1953

    Andrew Stewart   1953–5
        President of the New York State Society of Certified Public Ac-
        countants 1941–2.

               * Became partner in Haskins & Sells.

CANADIAN HEAD OFFICE. 1953 (*cont.*)

Walter J. Macdonald   1954–
    President of the Institute of Chartered Accountants of Manitoba
      1929–31; President of the Canadian Institute of Chartered
      Accountants 1953–4.

Ward W. McVey   1954–

MONTREAL. 1912

Vivian Harcourt (*see New York*)   1913–18
Gordon Tansley   1918–31
Campbell G. McConnell   1930–3
Kenneth W. Dalglish   1933–53
    President of the Dominion Association of Chartered Accountants
      1939–40 (now Canadian Institute of Chartered Account-
      ants); President of the Institute of Chartered Accountants of
      Province of Quebec 1935–6.

George P. Keeping (*see Toronto*)   1935–50
Robert C. Berry   1951–6
C. Donald Fraser   1953–
Peter S. Leggat   1953–
Harold S. Moffet (*see Regina*)   1956–

TORONTO. 1930

William J. Saunders   1930–43
William A. Cameron   1930–50
Gerald P. Strickland   1933–50
Edwin G. Gower   1943–50
George P. Keeping (*see Montreal*)   1950–2
Hartley R. Holmes   1951–
John R. Barker   1954–
Clem L. King   1955–
Hamish R. Macdonald (*see Windsor*)   1956–
John W. Bennett   1956–
Eddie C. Wilburn   1956–

VANCOUVER. 1953

William L. C. Wallace   1955–
Alan F. Sinclair   1955–
Clarence W. Duncan   1955–

WINNIPEG. 1954

George H. Carr	1954–
Frederic J. Tibbs	1954–
J. Francis Keeley	1954–
Peebles Kelly	1954–
Paul Kenway	1954–
G. Norman Wildgoose	1954–
Donald A. Tomlin	1954–
Arthur M. Tooley	1954–
Raymond A. Wildgoose	1954–

REGINA. 1955

Reginald R. Thomas 1955–
President of the Institute of Chartered Accountants of Saskatchewan 1934–6.

Harold S. Moffet (*see Montreal*) 1955–6
President of the Institute of Chartered Accountants of Saskatchewan 1951–2.

W. Givens Smith 1955–
President of the Institute of Chartered Accountants of Saskatchewan 1944–5; President of the Canadian Institute of Chartered Accountants 1956–7.

William M. Vicars 1955–
President of the Institute of Chartered Accountants of Saskatchewan 1948–9.

Clifford F. Westerman 1955–

PRINCE GEORGE. 1955

William R. M. Hollingshead 1955–

CALGARY. 1956

Ross H. Gould 1956–

EDMONTON. 1956

Harry O. Patriquin 1956–
President of the Institute of Chartered Accountants of Alberta 1925–6.

EDMONTON. 1956 *(cont.)*

James G. Duncan	1956–
President of the Institute of Chartered Accountants of Alberta *1948–9.*	
John P. McClary	1956–
President of the Institute of Chartered Accountants of Alberta *1956–7.*	
John E. Williams	1956–
J. Roy Leard	1956–
L. Stanley Pollard	1956–
Walter C. Howard	1956–
Keith C. Cardiff	1956–
Gordon A. R. Hauff	1956–.
Gordon F. McClary	1956–

WINDSOR. 1956

Hamish R. Macdonald *(see Toronto)*	1956–
Arthur M. Grainger	1956–
Joseph F. Tomsich	1956–

DELOITTE, PLENDER, GRIFFITHS & CO.	1914–25
DELOITTE, PLENDER, HASKINS & SELLS	1925–

CUBA

HAVANA. 1914

George Cochrane *(see New York)*	1918–21
Norman Newton	1921–7
William Eyre *(see New York)*	1926–7
George E. Green	1927–
Arthur E. L. Seymour	1946–50
Francis J. A. Wilkie	1946–
Edward H. B. Monck	1955–

DELOITTE, PLENDER, GRIFFITHS & CO.	1906–25
DELOITTE, PLENDER, HASKINS & SELLS	1925–

MEXICO

MEXICO CITY. 1906

Vivian Harcourt *(see Montreal)*	1911–13
Iver P. Thompson	1924–7
Anthony J. H. Thistlethwaite	1942–

DELOITTE, PLENDER, HASKINS & SELLS

PUERTO RICO

SAN JUAN. 1955

    William A. Waymouth   1955–

       President of the Puerto Rico Institute of Accountants 1932–7

       and in 1941.

    Fernando J. Domenech   1955–

    Glenn P. Leonard   1956–

South America

DELOITTE, DEVER, GRIFFITHS & CO.	In 1890's
DELOITTE, PLENDER, GRIFFITHS & CO.	1908–
and	
DELOITTE, PLENDER, HASKINS & SELLS	1930–

ARGENTINA

BUENOS AIRES. In 1890's
                1908

SUB-OFFICES:

TUCUMAN. 1912–38

ROSARIO. 1917

John Monteith Drysdale	1908–32
John A. Pilling*	1908–23
W. Snelson Bell, C.B.E.	1913–35
John J. Waite	1918–20
R. Glen Henderson	1918–21
Frederick T. Dickie	1921–9
Percy C. Stokes	1923–7
John A. McGlashan	1927–45
Alexander Rodger (*see West Coast*)	1929–36
Alexander Monteith Drysdale	1932–
Edward C. Richardson	1935–51
Arthur H. Beckett	1935–
Ninian L. Steel	1937–
Edward W. Johnson	1954–

* From 1923 to 1942 J. A. Pilling continued as a partner in the Argentine firm resident in London.

URUGUAY

MONTEVIDEO. 1921 (sub-office to Buenos Aires until 1950)

John C. Pert	1953–

DELOITTE, PLENDER, GRIFFITHS & CO.   1911–
and
DELOITTE, PLENDER, HASKINS, SELLS & CO.   1930–

BRAZIL

RIO DE JANEIRO. 1911

George L. Chandler	1914–37
Arthur C. Ciceri	1923–48
Vernon Smith	1937–
Bernard F. Stables (*see San Paulo*)	1946–50
	1956–
William S. B. Sampson	1948–55
Colin G. Stanbury	1951–
Henry W. Forbes (*see San Paulo*)	1955–6

RECIFE. 1917

Alfred J. Channon	1930–2

SAN PAULO. 1920

Bernard F. Stables (*see Rio de Janeiro*)	1950–6
John E. Jackson	1955–
Henry W. Forbes (*see Rio de Janeiro*)	1956–

SANTOS. 1921–33

PORTO ALEGRE. 1953

DELOITTE, PLENDER, GRIFFITHS & CO.   1921–
and
DELOITTE, PLENDER, HASKINS & SELLS   1930–

WEST COAST

CHILE

SANTIAGO DE CHILE. 1921

VALPARAISO. 1925

PERU

LIMA. 1925

AREQUIPA. 1952

John Dixon	1925–32
Thomas C. White, M.B.E.	1925–37

CHILI AND PERU (*cont.*)

Noel G. Ward		1925–41
Alexander Macdonald, C.B.E.		1925–48
Thomas M. Bury		1925–37
Alexander Rodger (*see Buenos Aires*)		1925–29
Geoffrey R. Bezer	Peru	1941–
William J. Webb	Peru	1948–
George Hopkinson	Chile	1948–
Oliver B. Simpson	Chile	1948–51
Thomas J. Foster Stuart	Chile	1952–

The practices of Deloitte & Co. and Sydney-Merritt & Co. were combined in 1925 under the name of Deloitte, Plender, Sydney-Merritt & Co. but in 1932 the name of Deloitte, Plender, Griffiths & Co. was resumed. As from 1948 separate firms were established in Peru and Chile.

DELOITTE, PLENDER, HASKINS & SELLS

VENEZUELA

CARACAS. 1955

Nathan McClure	1956–

COLOMBIA

MEDELLIN. 1956

Fergus M. Davidson	1956–

BOGOTA. 1956

Hugo Sanchez	1956–

Africa

DELOITTE, DEVER, GRIFFITHS, ANNAN & CO. 1904–11
DELOITTE, PLENDER, GRIFFITHS, ANNAN & CO. 1911–
and
DELOITTE, PLENDER, HASKINS & SELLS 1930–

UNION OF SOUTH AFRICA

JOHANNESBURG. 1904

Arthur N. Smith	1906–

President of the Transvaal Society of Accountants 1914–15.

Henry R. Brown	1919–23

JOHANNESBURG. 1904 (*cont.*)

Norman A. Stott (*see Bulawayo*)   1920–2
        1923–44

    President of the Transvaal Society of Accountants 1929–30.

Frank C. McConnell (*see Cape Town*)   1930–49
    President of the Transvaal Society of Accountants 1935–6.

Kenneth Lamont Smith   1936–
    President of the Transvaal Society of Accountants 1947–8.

Vivian M. Myburgh   1938–50
Douglas Lamont Smith   1944–
Norman Ross Lake (*see Durban*)   1949–
    President of the Transvaal Society of Accountants 1953–4.

B. Trouncer Downes   1949–
Charles R. Boden   1949–
Geoffrey J. D. Massey   1956–
Hugh A. Smith   1956–
Johannes S. K. Brink   1956–

CAPE TOWN. 1907

Alfred S. Hooper   1919–55
    *President of the Cape Society of Accountants and Auditors
    1937–40.*

Frank C. McConnell (*see Johannesburg*)   1930
John Hanson   1935–
Henry M. Bullen   1947–
Maurice A. Martin   1955
Norman C. Hartley   1956–

DURBAN. 1908

Alfred E. Hurley   1923–40
    *President of the Natal Society of Accountants 1921–2, 1929–
    30, and 1934–5.*

Norman Ross Lake (*see Johannesburg*)   1936–49
    *President of the Natal Society of Accountants 1944–5 and
    1948–9.*

Clement D. Ramsden   1947–
    President of the Natal Society of Accountants 1951–2.

C. Crawford Erwin   1948–

PORT ELIZABETH. 1929
    Denis G. Brittain   1944–53
    C. Gordon Reeler   1953–

PIETERMARITZBURG. 1936
    C. B. Ibbetson Porter   1941–
      President of the Natal Society of Accountants 1953–4.

EAST LONDON. 1938
    Philip W. Westerton   1944–

FEDERATION OF RHODESIA AND NYASALAND

SOUTHERN RHODESIA

BULAWAYO. 1905
    Hugh T. Guerrier   1912–22
                                             1923–6
    Norman A. Stott (*see Johannesburg*)   1922–3
    Charles J. MacNaughtan   1926–48
      President of the Rhodesia Society of Accountants 1929–30 and 1939–40.
    Walter D. Goodwin   1940–6
    Alan Underwood   1943–
      President of the Rhodesia Society of Accountants 1950–1.
    Brian L. Sedgwick   1947–
    Frank E. Sweetman   1955–

SALISBURY. 1910
    C. Roberts Musto   1931–
      President of the Rhodesia Society of Accountants 1933–4 and 1951–2.
    Cecil F. Buckland   1940–
    Brian W. S. O'Connell   1950–
    Anthony J. Pickett   1955–

GWELO. 1955
    Charles R. B. C. Stephan (*see Lusaka*)   1955–

UMTALI. 1950

NORTHERN RHODESIA

NDOLA. 1931
    Robert A. T. Fookes   1940–

LUSAKA. 1950
    Charles R. B. C. Stephan (*see Gwelo*)   1953–5

KITWE. 1952
    Alan Spedding   1952–

NYASALAND

LIMBE. 1932–3

BLANTYRE. 1948
    J. L. Rowland Brown   1954–

        DELOITTE, PLENDER, GILL & JOHNSON   1949–
                      and
        DELOITTE, PLENDER, HASKINS & SELLS   1954–

KENYA

NAIROBI. 1949
    Ernest B. Gill   1949–51
    P. James Gill   1949–
    Edward P. Johnson   1949–
    Harold E. Gill   1949–50
    Peter M. Johnson   1949–
    John G. Highwood   1951–
    David G. R. Carter   1955–

MOMBASA. 1952

TANGANYIKA

DAR-ES-SALAAM. 1949

IRINGA. 1954

MBEYA. 1957

UGANDA

KAMPALA. 1952

Australia

DELOITTE, PLENDER, GRIFFITHS & CO.

MELBOURNE. 1949

George Sutherland Smith   1949–

President of the Victorian State Council of the Institute of Chartered Accountants in Australia 1949; President of the General Council of the Institute of Chartered Accountants in Australia 1952.

Thomas W. McMahon   1949–

John A. Hepworth   1952–

SYDNEY. 1949

Charles N. Campbell   1949–

Hill W. Mackisack   1949–

Francis M. D. Jackett   1949–

Clifford A. Rush   1949–

Asia

DELOITTE, PLENDER, TOUCHE & CO.

JAVA. 1910–1915

BATAVIA

SURABAYA

DELOITTE, PLENDER, HASKINS & SELLS

JAPAN

TOKYO. 1955

Edward L. Carey   1955–

INDEX

Johnson, Edward W., 154.
Johnson, Peter M., 159.
Joint Stock Companies, 2, 13.
Joynson-Hicks, M.P., 104.

Kampala Office, 90, 159.
Keeley, J. Francis, 152.
Keeping, George P., 151.
Kelly, Peebles, 152.
Kenway, Paul, 152.
Kenya Offices, 90, 159.
Kerr, Robert, xi, 107.
Kettle, Richard, xi, 137.
Kettle, Russell (Sir Russell Kettle), ix, xi, 110, 122, 127, 132, 134, 138, 139, 142, 143, 144, 147.
Kilpatrick, James, ix, xi, 1, 12, 91, 110, 137.
King, Clem L., 151.
King Edward's Hospital Fund for London, 76.
King George's Fund for Sailors, 114.
King George's Jubilee Trust, 114.
Kitwe Office, 89, 159.
Knollys, The Viscount, G.C.M.G., M.B.E., D.F.C., 146.
Kylsant, Lord, 119.

Laenderbank, 100.
Lake, N. Ross, 157.
Lancashire & Cheshire Telephone Co., 40.
Lancashire & Yorkshire Railway, 11, 20, 24, 30.
Langham Hotel, 63.
Law Guarantee Trust & Accident Society Ltd., 98.
Lawson, W. H., C.B.E., 149.
Leaf, Walter, 102.
Lean, Walter, 46.
Leard, J. Roy, 153.

Leggat, Peter S., 151.
Leonard, Glenn P., 154.
Letter Books of 1854–8 and 1887–8, 11, 44.
Lever Brothers Ltd., 92.
Lima Office, 94, 155.
Limbe Office, 89, 159.
Limited Liability, 13, 66.
Lofoten Islands, 53.
Loit or Loitte Grand and Petit, 10.
London & River Plate Bank, 15, 46.
London Assurance, 109.
London, Chatham & Dover Railway, 40.
Londonderry family, 11.
London Electricity Board, 134.
London Joint Stock Bank, 66.
London Passenger Transport Board, 87.
London transport, 86.
London Transport Executive, 87.
London Wall Buildings, No. 5, 78, 131.
Lord, Frank A., xi, 133.
Los Angeles Office, 48, 150.
Lothbury Cricket Club, 80.
Lothbury, No. 4, 12, 36, 79.
Lothbury Road, Johannesburg, 89.
Louette St. Denis and St. Pierre, 10.
Lowe, E. Norman, 148.
Luff, R. E. R., 115.
Lusaka Office, 89, 158.

McClary, Gordon F., 153.
McClary, John P., 153.
McClure, Nathan, 156.
McConnell, Campbell G., 151.
McConnell, Frank C., 157.
Macdonald, Alexander, C.B.E., 155.
Macdonald & Healy, 142.
Macdonald, Hamish R., 151, 153.
Macdonald, John H., 90.
Macdonald, Walter J., 142, 151.
McGeachy, Edward A., 148.
McGlashan, John A., 154.

Macgregor, James P., 150.
McGrigor & Co., Sir Charles, 112–13.
McKenna, Rt. Hon. Reginald, P.C., 111.
Mackisack, Hill W., 160.
Maclaren, Goode & Co., 48.
McMahon, Thomas W., 160.
McNamara, William R., 149.
MacNaughton, Charles J., 158.
McPhail, Robert T. M., M.B.E., xi, 137, 144, 148.
Macqueen-Pope, W., 41.
McVey, Ward W., 151.
Maltby, Lionel, xi, 76, 87, 100, 110, 114.
Managers, 69.
Manchester & Liverpool District Bank (District Bank), 20.
Manchester Office, 20, 138, 147.
Manchester Society of Accountants, 7.
March, R. H., 54.
Marconi-Wireless Telegraph Co. Ltd., 115.
Martin, Maurice A., 157.
Martin, Richard C., xi, 108, 110.
Massey, Geoffrey J. D., 157.
May Consolidated Gold Mining Co. Ltd., 80.
Mbeya Office, 90, 159.
Medellin Office (Colombia), 141, 156.
Meister, Lucius & Bruning Ltd., 104.
Melbourne Office, 142, 159–60.
Melnotte, Miss (Royal Comedy Theatre, Haymarket), 60.
Metcalf, Graeme M., 147.
Metropolitan Life Assurance Society, 56.
Metropolitan Water Board, 86.
Mexico City Office, 90, 116, 153.
Midlands, work in, 53.
Milan Office, 115, 148.
Millar Macdonald & Co., 141.
Ministry of Transport and Civil Aviation, 86.
Moffet, Harold S., 151, 152.

Mombassa Office, 90, 159.
Monck, Edward H. B., 153.
Monkhouse, G. B., 74.
Montevideo Office, 94, 155.
Montreal Office, 48, 151.
Morrish, Gordon E., xi, 137.
Moscow Office, 91, 149.
Murietta & Co. Ltd., 72, 73.
Murray, George S., 148.
Musto, C. Roberts, 158.
Myburgh, Vivian M., 157.

Nairobi Office, 90, 159.
National Debt of United Kingdom, 1900–55, 145.
National Dock Labour Board, 134.
National Economy Committee, 118.
National Expenditure of the United Kingdom, 1900–55, 145.
National Insurance Act, 97.
Nationalization Policy, 133.
National Telephone Company, 40.
Navy, Army & Air Force Institutes (N.A.A.F.I.), 105.
Ndola Office, 89, 158.
Nevsky Prospect, St. Petersburg, 91.
Newgate Prison, 3.
New Jersey Transport Organization, 86.
Newton, Norman, 153.
New York Office, 48, 106.
Nigerian Government, 143.
Nitrate Railways Co. Ltd., 55.
Northcliffe, Lord, 101–3.
Northern Ireland, work in, 99.
Nyasaland Offices, 89, 159.

Observer, 61.
Ocean Coal Co. Ltd., 15.
O'Connell, Brian W. S., 158.
Office discipline, 66.
Office functions, 83–85.
Office Rules and Regulations, 68.

PRINTED IN
GREAT BRITAIN
AT THE
UNIVERSITY PRESS
OXFORD
BY
CHARLES BATEY
PRINTER
TO THE
UNIVERSITY